NADIA

Nadia

The Autobiography of
NADIA COMANECI

PROTEUS BOOKS
LONDON/NEW YORK

PROTEUS BOOKS
is an imprint of the
Proteus Publishing Group

United States
PROTEUS PUBLISHING CO., INC.
733 Third Avenue
New York, NY 10017
distributed by
THE SCRIBNER BOOK COMPANIES, INC.
597 Fifth Avenue
New York, NY 10017
United Kingdom
PROTEUS (PUBLISHING) LIMITED
Bremar house
Sale Place
London W2 1PT

ISBN
0 906071 56 9 *paperback*
0 906071 78 X *cased*

First published 1981

Printed in Great Britain by
Anchor Press Limited, and bound by
Wm. Brendon & Son Limited, both of
Tiptree, Colchester, Essex

For my family

Acknowledgements

Nadia's horoscope was compiled by
Ann Petrie
Shambhala
10 South Moulton Street
London W1Y 1DF

Pictures
Alan E. Burrows
Sports Agence Magazines, Paris
Graham Buxton Smither

Sportal, Bucharest
and from Nadia's personal collection

Contents

Introduction

I SUPPOSE that it must seem precocious and a little arrogant for someone who is not yet 20 years old to attempt to write her autobiography, but having been asked to do so, it has proved a rewarding experience. In such a short span of time, years during which most youngsters are just preparing for life, an awful lot has happened to me and those around me and there have been some amazing stories told and printed about me, nearly all of them somewhat off the mark.

In Romania, I don't often read the newspapers and magazines from across the world and so I'm blissfully ignorant of most of what is written about me. It is only when I get the chance to sit down and read some of the thousands of letters that arrive weekly at the Gymnastics Federation Office in central Bucharest that some of these weird stories and descriptions come to light. It is very obvious from the letters I get that many of my supporters who write are often as concerned as I am about something that I am supposed to have said or done. The crazy nature of some of these things never ceases to amaze me, and why and how they have come to be written remains a mystery.

Within the space of a few weeks, I find out that I am overweight, underweight, suffering from hypnotic control, suffering from the use of proscribed drugs; according to the press I have retired a dozen times and on one serious occasion, I had apparently attempted suicide after a broken love affair with some elderly poet! Although some of these statements are laughable, some can be, and have been, deeply wounding. Usually, it's only through the upsetting effect such remarks have on my fans that I get to hear of them. On one memorable day, I was suffering from anorexia according to a report in a Japanese newspaper, and struggling to keep my weight down according to a French paper, both at the same time! That afternoon, the Federation received a telephone call from an American press agency asking what I was going to do now that I had announced my retirement from the sport. One of the problems of this sort of situation is that if I responded to every error in the foreign press, I would have no time left to train, let alone compete!

The press made too much of our success at the Montreal Olympics and since then, they have given me little cause to trust and respect them. At times, I feel that the press and television are partly responsible for my success; that they have "created" a celebrity called Nadia Comaneci and have, therefore, the right to exploit her. Here in Eastern Europe, we are particularly easy prey; because we are often unaware of what the papers say, we can't deny the stories and so they go unchallenged. Fortunately, we have a few selfless friends in the West who have been determined to get to the bottom of some of the more unpleasant things that have been said, but sometimes the damage is already done. I suppose it is inevitable that the media does not devote the same energy and enthusiasm to publicizing corrections as they do to publishing controversial rumors and speculation.

One of the most distressing things was receiving letters from parents who were unable to comfort their unhappy children after the 'news' of my 'suicide attempt'. Many of them felt that I had betrayed them and their children and thought that the pressures of the sport had become inhuman. A lot of harm had been done as a result of an unfounded and malicious story. What can we do? Well, this book is part of the answer. As someone who is in the public eye I have to expect a bit of rough treatment along with the smooth from the press – and I must admit I have received more then my fair share of plaudits – but particularly because gymnastics is appealing more and more to very young, impressionable kids I consider it important to set the record straight. So many of my supporters and, more importantly, my friends had urged me to reply to the many allegations, that when I was offered the chance to write this book, I leapt at it.

In a way I am my own worst enemy when it comes to public relations. Often, when inane or loaded questions are thrown at me by the press, I just clam up, which is probably why I am known as "little Miss Perfect", "the ice-queen", "the gym-machine" etc., perhaps with some justification, though I like to think that the real me is rather different from the public image.

The most difficult thing about writing a book about myself is that the whole thing seems terribly egotistical. I have spent much of my competitive life trying to avoid being the center of the media's attention by emphasizing that I have always been part of a team. The first person singular is still uncomfortable to use, but my best friend, Anca Grigoras, has helped me lose some of my self-consciousness.

One of the best things about writing this book has been the perspective it has given me on the present state of gymnastics. Anca, who is 4 years older, has been competing internationally for longer than me and I have the greatest respect for her observations and opinions. It was Anca who pointed out how much gymnastics has changed – even since I first became involved at international level.

Olga Korbut burst onto the scene in the 1972 Munich Olympics and drastically changed the whole sport. Her instant appeal and popularity brought gymnastics into the public eye, and suddenly every girl wanted to be another Olga. With the explosion of interest came inevitable problems. There just wasn't the machinery to cope with the sudden increase in major international competitions. It put too much pressure on the relatively small number of top-class gymnasts, coaches, judges and facilities. Corners are now being cut, and occasionally, safety regulations and Competition rules are being flouted in order to "give the public what it wants".

As a competitor, and now as a student coach, I must confess that I am worried about the future of this precious sport. My anxiety is confined largely to the women's event, for it is here that the greatest changes have taken place. There is so much "national" prestige at stake among the leading countries, putting a heavy responsibility on even the youngest of the hopefuls, aged around 6 or 7. It just doesn't seem right for a child of this age to have to face such savage discipline and grueling training schedules for the sake of her country. Fortunately, though, there is now a tendency in sports schools in Romania to start out with play-gymnastics for those youngsters who have the talent to progress to Competition standard.

Perhaps one of the most worrying things about gymnastics now is the element of risk that has to be included in routines. Anca said in a recent chat that she no longer enjoys watching a major competition. 'Even during a competition I could relax between events by watching the others, but now, in the voluntaries, I am terrified at what might happen to some of the youngest girls. It's more like a circus than a sport.'

In the last five years, technical complexity has come to matter more than artistic expression. To a certain extent, I feel responsible for this. In gymnastics, girls tend to be modeled on the current leading personality. This started with Olga; suddenly coaches were looking for carbon-copy Korbuts with the result that the "gamines" took over. These little girls won the hearts of their audiences; there were a few risky elements, but, in my view, the sport had lost its way. It had degenerated into a showbiz spectacle. True, there were still competitors like Tourischeva to lend it dignity and grace, but their days were definitely numbered.

Our team's Montreal success brought about another turn-around in the sport: technical virtuosity became the order-of-the-day. However, this was the result on our part of years of intensive preparation, which some coaches and parents failed to appreciate. Suddenly, they started pushing the younger gymnasts too far, too fast. Many people instituted training systems that they mistakenly thought were along the same lines as our own, with the result that the world witnessed a lot of diminutive, serious faced gymnastic machines parading as competitors. And who got the blame for this? Me and my coach during this period, Bela Karoly. We can't reasonably be held to blame for the actions of our imitators.

As I matured physically, it was inevitable that the style and content of my exercises should change. The many problems that this caused will be discussed later, but suffice to say that at the first sign of *progressing*, I started to get written off as a competitor, because I no longer resembled my media image. Only after the dust from Moscow had settled did the "new Nadia" receive a measure of acceptance.

I would actually welcome gymnasts following the example of the "new Nadia". For, with my new shape and style, and those of some of my fellow competitors and rivals who are all about the same age, we are now in a position to allow the sport to revert to a greater classicism which would take a lot of pressure away from the juniors. The recent decision to raise the age limit for competing at senior level has been a first step in the right direction. I am aware that my generation of gymnasts has a great responsibility to the future of our sport.

As I hope you will see during the course of this book, there is much more that is good about gymnastics than is bad, and equally, there has been a lot more in my life so far to remember fondly than to be concerned about. It was not something that I was aware of until I sat down and started to write. With the help of Anca and "our Englishman", working on this autobiography has been great fun.

I suppose I should introduce you briefly to "our Englishman" and his role in this venture. Graham Buxton Smither came to see me in Romania in April, 1978, the first of many such visits. When I left to go back to Deva with Bela, he continued to travel to Bucharest to meet with other gymnasts, write the occasional article and take hundreds of photographs. He soon became a familiar figure in the training halls and at the Sports Ministry. It was a new experience to find someone who was genuinely concerned for us as people. In 1980 he wrote a book on the world of gymnastics, and I was delighted to write the foreword to it. Later, he came over in response to some mistaken press reports about myself and my teammates and then suggested that the only way to clear things up was for me to commit myself to paper. Initially, it was just a throw-away comment, but after more discussion and thought, the idea began to grow in appeal. Graham's agreement to help in the production of the manuscript was what finally made it all possible.

1

BENDING DOWN on the Moscow victory rostrum, my eye caught the glint of the silver medal before the ribbon was placed around my neck. I was vaguely aware of the loud applause from the audience and after receiving the medal and all the usual kisses I turned to congratulate Elena Davydova who had won the Overall Competition. At the same time, Maxi Gnauck was presented with her joint silver and once again there was a loud burst of applause from the auditorium. I felt miles away from the public; I was filled with a detached exhaustion and emptiness after the competition. As I stared blankly at the raising of flags, half hearing the Soviet national anthem blaring through the public address system, my main thought was: how fast can I get out of the arena and find myself some ice-cream? It was only this that gave me the strength to face the hoards of press photographers until our final escape from the hall in the bus, back to the Village. Would there be any chocolate ice-cream? One of the fondest memories for me of the Moscow Olympics is the quality of the ice-cream and all the incredible range of flavors!

What a day it had been! When I woke up on that fateful morning, I had a feeling I would be better off staying in bed. My back was hurting me a lot, because for some time now I had been suffering from sciatica which made strong movements of my legs quite painful – hardly the sort of problem you need when competing anywhere, let alone at the Olympics. Bela, the team coach, and the team doctor popped their heads around the door and were greeted by the sight of three bleary-eyed gymnasts peering at them.

'Come on, get up. Breakfast is in half an hour and the bus leaves for training at eight. Nadia, how is your back this morning?' Before I could reply, Bela snapped at the others in the room to hurry up; it was obvious that he had made the same calculations as us during the night and knew that it would be an uphill struggle to win the Overall medal. Dana (better known as Dumitrita Turner), who is the clown of the team and World Vault Champion, and I had sat up until about one o'clock trying to work out whether or not the judges would be fair to us now that the Russians had gotten the Team gold medal. In view of the previous marking, neither of us was over confident. Bela's nervousness was general that day, it infected the whole team.

The atmosphere in our group's apartment was tense at the best of times, partly because Bela and Marta insisted on the virtual isolation of the girls from the rest of the Village. I was fortunate in spending much of the time with Nicu, our Secretary General and so I was able to get about more than the others. It is difficult to describe adequately what it feels like to be cooped up in team quarters throughout the period of a competition as lengthy and important as the Olympics. We did not get to go out, to let off steam in one of the discos, or to meet socially with some of the other contestants. Inevitably, frustration tends to build up at times, tensions and rivalries bubble to the surface. Luckily, most of the Romanian girls are old friends, although since I no longer train with them in Deva, some of my teammates have a tendency to regard me rather jealously, particularly when my back is turned. This sort of wrangling is common in most teams, inevitable really among dedicated and talented competitors, each of whom wants to be number one. Provided it is out in the open, it can be channelled into healthy competitiveness. But when it is suppressed, it does no one any good.

As a team, we had not been enjoying a good competition. Our greatest problem quite apart from our personal doubts was the judging itself. We found ourselves nominated into an unfavorable group, separated from our true rivals, the Soviet Union and East Germany, who were competing together. Although some of our girls made some unnecessary errors, most independent observers seemed to feel that we were being deliberately down-marked. During the floor exercise in the Team Competition, one of the Scientific and Technical Collaborators came up to me, shrugged her shoulders and said in poor English, 'What can I say? I record all the elements and series, the judges don't consult me and the agreed score is a joke. What can I do? Only when there is a protest can I help.' Her apologetic manner had turned to one of frustrated anger. I replied simply, 'We expected nothing less, it's our problem.' A resigned smile crossed her face and with a heartfelt 'Good luck', she left the arena. That little meeting said it all.

The result of the Team event was that we maintained our position reached at Montreal, which gave us the silver medal. I cannot say whether the final positions would have been different without some of the more dubious judging, for any of the top three teams were in with a

18

chance of taking the gold.

One of the sad things about competing is that you miss almost everything else that is going on in the Hall. Total concentration is required throughout the time that you are in the arena, so you are unaware of other athletes' performances. One momentary lapse can cost you the lot, which brings me to the painful memory of my fall from the bars at the end of the Team competition.

I shall start to take it personally if I have many more disasters on the asymmetric bars, for they are my favorite piece of apparatus. At the Strasbourg World Championships in 1978, I'd managed to fall from them, and once again, here we all were at a major competition, and the same thing happens. I know consistency is supposed to be my hallmark, but consistency of this sort I can live without!

To my great surprise, lots of people found excuses for my Moscow fall, though Bela was certainly not one of them. When I had restarted the exercise, completed it, and dismounted from the podium, Bela was nowhere to be seen. The moment I fell, he turned his back in a public display of disgust. I can't say that I blame him for it because I was pretty sick about it myself. There was a deathly hush throughout the auditorium, a stunned silence, and at times like that you realize how exposed and vulnerable you are, alone on the rostrum and with the eyes of the world upon you.

The Code of Points, which is the judging manual, states that a gymnast has a maximum of thirty seconds in which to resume the exercise after a fall, otherwise it is considered as finished. So what else was there to do but get up and continue? What made the whole thing more galling was that when the slip happened, the routine was nearly finished anyway, and worst of all, it was such a simple element that caused my downfall. If it had come during the Comaneci somersault, it might have been more pardonable.

More than my dignity had been bruised in that fall, and as I gingerly made my way back to the bench, I was half aware of the sympathetic stares from some of my fellow competitors. At first I felt angry, and then strangely numb, until I sat down when I was furious with myself. Not only had I let myself down, but I knew the sorrow that would be in the hearts of many of my countrymen back home, watching their televisions. There was no one to blame but me. I had broken my golden rule; I had allowed my concentration to drift. It was for no more than a split second, but that was enough.

Afterwards, my many supporters were quick to rush to my defense, their most usual comment being, 'It was that damned idiot with the flash-gun, wasn't it!' I only wish it had been. It would have been wonderful to be able to blame somebody else. The truth is that I can't remember noticing a bright flash in my eyes during the exercise. In the video replay of the incident, I could see that someone fired a flash at the critical moment. The excuse was certainly up for grabs but I'm afraid it would not have been the truth. My back *was* hurting me at the time, but again, I don't seriously believe that it played any part in my failure. Why did my concentration waver? I doubt that I will ever know. I can only say that it did, and that I paid the full price.

The matter was hardly mentioned by Marta and Bela. The other girls, though, were nearly as upset as me. I was there in Moscow to defend my Overall Gold from Montreal and, in one brief moment, the chance to win any medal at all had threatened to slip from my grasp. When I first arrived at the Games, I didn't think I stood a chance of winning a medal because the sciatica had forced me to drop several of the more demanding new elements from my work. Now through sheer bloody-mindedness, I had worked myself into a position where a gold medal was a possibility, and then chucked it all away. Actually, just writing about it now makes me angry all over again!

By that evening, I could see things in a better light. All I had done was to show that I was human and therefore fallible. And thus it was that Dana and I sat up that night working out the various possibilities, nibbling at titbits that I had managed to sneak past our team officials. We had to keep our voices as low as possible so as not to bring any one into the room during our midnight feast. We gossiped about our opponents, pulled them all to bits and ended up in a heap of giggles. I suppose it was a reaction to all the stresses. Sleep that night was short, but deep.

And so it was, half asleep and with a painful back, that I crawled out of that lovely warm bed, to lift myself for the day's Overall Final.

The situation going into this final was that after the Team Voluntary Exercises were completed, the leading individuals were placed in the following order:

1:	Maxi Gnauck	GDR	79·35
2:	Natalia Shaposhnikova	USSR	79·15
3:	Emilia Eberle	Romania	79·10
4:	Nadia Comaneci	Romania	79·05
5:	Elena Davydova	USSR	79·00

You can see that my teammate Emilia was ahead of me, and Maxi was the person who had made the greatest progress since the Team Compulsories, for there she was placed behind Natalia and myself. Even at this stage, Elena Davydova was breathing down my neck. To be honest, I have never worried about names and reputations when competing in gymnastics. In a fair and open event, it does not matter who the opponents are. So long as the judging and organization are entirely sound, there is only one person who can affect my performance and that is me.

After Bela and the doctor had finished with me, I had to endure the agonies of physiotherapy on my back, which, by the time I arrived at the training hall, was feeling far less painful. Although there were only three competitors from each team allowed into Competition II, as stipulated in the Code of Points, our whole team took the opportunity of working out. Emilia, Rodica Dunca, and I were through to the day's event and we were allowed by Bela and Marta to monopolize all the apparatus. Bela and I came to an understanding in Bucharest, during the three days that he and his girls were there prior to the departure for Moscow, that he would not involve himself in any coaching unless I asked him. 'Don't worry, I know exactly what to do. The best thing is to leave me alone to get on with it. If I need help, I'll ask for it, OK?', I said to him in a quiet moment during his first squad session. 'That's OK with me,' he replied, and so we got on just fine in training. We respected each other and there were no heavy confrontations.

During that morning's effort, it became apparent that Bela had come to the decision that the best prospect for one of the Individual Overall medals lay in my performance. It was all down to temperament and consistency, and it is here that he feels I am strongest. The problem was that if I was to have anything more than an outside chance of a medal, my fellow contestants had to make mistakes similar to my earlier classic on the bars. Would they be obliging? Remembering my previous night's conversation with Dana, I felt some of them could be expected to wilt under the pressure of the event, which would let me in with a mathematical chance. As for Emilia, who was placed ahead of me, she was in no way going to help me get on to the winners' rostrum, least of all at her expense – and who could blame her? I'd have felt exactly the same way in her place. It was just the kind of situation that highlights the quality of the team coach and reveals if he or she feels any favoritism!

Late that day, we found ourselves back in the hall waiting for the competition to begin. Little did we realize what a storm was in store for the beam and the gymnastics world at the end of that evening. As usual, I can't remember much about my actual performance. The only thing I keep close tabs on is the scoring, and what I need to achieve in order to win. Some people think that this creates impossible pressure, but I find I am much happier and perform better with a precise personal target. When I told Anca this, she said, 'I could never do that, I don't want to know what my opponents are doing, it would make me nervous. The only time I check the scores is after the whole thing is over. As long as my exercises are all right, that's all I need to know. I'm not like you, I just take each exercise as it comes.'

During the course of the Final, I realized that Natalia and Emilia were slipping from their earlier positions and interestingly, Elena Davydova was coming up fast into medal contention. Maxi was the one that I thought I'd have to beat, so Elena's performance was quite a surprise to me. What was an even bigger surprise was that I found myself with a chance for the gold. As I suggested earlier, it was due as much to the mistakes made by the others as my own work. Even if I'd picked up a ten on every piece of apparatus, I could not have gotten into the medals unless the other competitors lost points.

In contrast to the previous day, I was performing well. The judges awarded me a perfect score on the asymmetric bars. Despite all the earlier judging problems, I was actually in a position to strike for the gold. Like all the best (or worst!) fiction, everything hinged on the last piece of apparatus, and guess who was lumbered with the position as final competitor? Maxi had secured a silver medal with her bars work and Elena's excellent floor exercise had placed her in the gold medal position. The only competitor capable of upsetting this cosy little arrangement was me. It was all down to the beam exercise.

I had been keeping an eye on the other routines on the beam, and had carefully noted the way the judges had been marking. What struck me was not just the deductions that the panel was making for minor faults, but also their interpretation of the bonus points available for the risk element on moves of superior difficulty. In gymnastics, each part of an exercise is given a grade of difficulty. They are 'A', 'B', and 'C', the last being the toughest and therefore deserving the highest mark. However, by adding additional risks to one of the 'C' rated moves, there is an additional maximum of 0.20 points available.

Everybody had made several minor errors and the judges seemed to feel that many of the routines contained elements of risk. I knew that a flawless performance should give me the first place. A couple of very minor errors, according to the results of the previous competitors, should still leave me with a good chance. However, the fact that I was the last and that it was a Soviet gymnast who was placed in the gold slot just before me nagged at my mind. All I could do was my best.

During my exercise, I made two minor mistakes, both of which were tiny breaks of form. There was half a wobble after a combination on the beam, and my feet were not quite together on landing. Now, if I had to judge that performance, and I awarded marks according to the letter of the law, I would have given a score of 9·80. To win the Overall Individual Title, I needed 9·95. However, we had all seen the earlier scores which were in some cases more than a little lenient, so maybe I could still get away with it. In my mind, though, the moment I made the second error I knew that the judges had the perfect excuse to deny me the gold, and with Maxi in the silver position, perhaps that too. A Romanian woman, Maria Simionescu (better known to every one as Mili) was the Head Judge of my final piece. As the First Vice President of the Women's Technical Committee of the International Gymnastics Federation, she had devoted much time to the new Code of Points, and she, if anyone, would know the rules.

Bela and Marta were there to greet me after my dismount, and he made a big show of hugging me, seeming confident of a Romanian victory. I was less sure. A quick glance in the direction of the judging panel confirmed my suspicions – there was a Judges' Conference. Bela, and by this time Geza Poszar, our choreographer, were standing behind them watching the score sheets. Suddenly, Bela exploded with rage and started a violent argument with one of the judges. The marks that were given by the four adjudicators were: 10·00. 9·90, 9·80, 9·80. Knock off the top and bottom marks, and average the two remaining scores and you get the final mark, in this case 9·85. But, in view of the earlier scores, Mili could not understand why I was singled out by two of the members of that panel for a stricter application of the rules. I could see that two of the judges were arguing with the other two, who certainly did not look as if they were prepared to reconsider their mark. Bela was not making matters any easier by intimidating one of them. I guessed my cause was lost.

I stood quietly, well away from the fray, simply waiting to find out whether I had also lost the silver. The hall was now in uproar. Mili, as Head Judge, had said that she would not be a party to what she considered an injustice and invited Ellen Berger, President of the Women's Technical Committee to put up the score herself. My thoughts ran back to 1977 and the incident during the Prague European Championships. The same people were involved here – Mili Simionescu, Ellen Berger of East Germany, and Yuri Titov of the USSR, who is the President of the International Gymnastics Federation (FIG). On that occasion, which I deal with later in the book, the Romanian Team was recalled home because it was obvious to everyone that we were not going to receive fair treatment. Nelli Kim and I were the unwitting pawns in that particular power struggle.

Now, gymnastics was witnessing the embarrassing spectacle of the three most senior members of the FIG in disagreement over the marks that had been awarded to their respective nationals. I could hear shouts of 'Fair-play' being directed at the Jury of Appeal from the auditorium. Mili and Ellen Berger were shuttling to and fro between the Jury and the Beam Panel. Bela and Geza were protesting furiously. The Russian team was fidgeting nervously. My teammates were sitting impatiently and cursing the judges. I was hungry. Having been tipped that the score was 9·85, and feeling sure that it would not change, I had calculated that that would give me a joint silver with Maxi. That being the case, my mind naturally wandered to the more serious matter of where my next ice-cream was coming from!

After 27 minutes of heated, and largely futile, debate, an impartial official was called on to put up the score of 9·85. Bela made his feelings plain, in a gesture purely for the public eye, by spitting in the direction of the judges and gesticulating wildly at an imagined foe. He was the picture of injured innocence! This part of the Olympic gymnastics competition was over. There was just the medal ceremony to be endured, and then we could leave. Thus it was that I ended up with the silver medal around my neck. It was back to the restaurant, at long last.

Little was said about the whole incident when we got back to the apartment. To be honest, we were all too exhausted even to think about it. I slept long and deeply that night, which was just as well for I was through to the Apparatus Finals, and had a good chance of picking up something on the beam and the floor. I was more than hopeful of taking the beam gold. Perhaps some of the disappointments of one day could be wiped out on another.

Lifting our spirits and snapping into the right frame of mind for the second set of finals was a tough challenge. There was a feeling of despondency in the camp after the earlier judging problems; would they recur in this last series of exercises? The only sure route to a medal was to be perfect. At the top level of many sports, gymnastics included, the psychological demands are greater than the physical. Singleminded determination and total self-control give you the edge in a close fight. We had a good team talk (at least I think it was good because I can't remember a word of it!) that boosted team morale tremendously.

Self-motivation is very much the key to the many hours of hard work I have put into gymnastics and the successes that I have gotten out of it. This stems partly from my own character and also from the experiences of my childhood. It is only since writing this book that I have come to realize how many of my current traits and characteristics can be traced back to my childhood. It is also very easy to see how I came to love gymnastics, even before I knew what it was.

2

NADIA IS not a typical Romanian name; indeed, until quite recently, it was very rare indeed. So how did my mother and father come to choose such a name for their daughter? It seems that at the time when they knew that my mother was going to have a baby later that year, they went to the movies, to celebrate the good news. It was a Russian film, and the heroine was called Nadia, which is a shortened form of the name Nadejda, and my mother was so taken with the character that she decided that if she had a girl, that would be her name. Incidentally, the name means 'hope'. My father was hoping for a son, and would have called him Adrian.

And so, on November 12, 1961, Nadia Elena Comaneci made her loud entrance into the world and my father, Gheorghe, instantly forgave Stefania, my mother, for producing a daughter. Six years later, all my father's hopes were realized when my brother was born and, of course, he was named Adrian.

Romania is a country that the world beyond its borders knows little about, so forgive me if at this stage I give it a brief plug. There is no country that I love more or, despite frequent travels, have found more beautiful. It is a land of great contrasts, from the enormous, flat-reed-covered Danube delta to the staccato buttresses of the Carpathian mountains. In the south and south-east, the land is very fertile and forms an enormous plain which is heavily farmed. In the north and north-west, we are protected by the Transylvanian Alps and huge forests of fir trees. We are also very fortunate in having the beautiful Black Sea coast to our east, which is where I go for a holiday every summer.

In many parts of the countryside, time seems to move at a leisurely pace, in contrast to the hustle and bustle of the big cities and industrial areas. Romania has one of of the highest industrial growth rates of any country in the world and new petrochemical, mining, and engineering

25

plants are being developed all the time. There is a huge contrast in the types of architecture to be found. The monasteries of Moldavia, with their external paintings of religious scenes could not be further removed from the ultra-modern designs of buildings like the Palace of Sport and Culture in Bucharest. Traditional styles, whether of clothes or buildings, or whatever, reflect one of the characteristics of our people – a love of decoration.

The Romanian is a Latin by temperament and origin, being descended from the Dacians. Generally, we are lively, gregarious, and extrovert and are as dedicated to enjoying life to the full as anyone. Although those of us committed to gymnastics have to control some of our wilder traits – sometimes! – I like to think that the joy that lies deep within the Romanian soul shows occasionally in our expressiveness during a performance that is really going well.

The town in which I lived throughout my childhood is called Gheorghe Gheorghiu-Dej, (after the first President of the Socialist Republic of Romania), but it is still generally known by its old name of Onesti. It used to be a small foresting village, before the program of industrialization started. It is cradled in the foothills of the Carpathian Mountains within Moldavia, one of the most beautiful provinces in Romania. The people of this province have a reputation for being the kindest and most hospitable in our country. It is a magical place, and I have always felt lucky that I was born there.

If ever a child aged its parents overnight, it was me. They must have had incredible patience because I was virtually uncontrollable. As soon as I had the strength to rock my crib or carriage I went at it with a vengeance, or so my parents told me, and I believe them. I was bursting both with energy and curiosity. From the moment I was able to crawl, life became one great exploration of unknown places. I can vaguely remember when time after time, a brief expedition into the wilds of the kitchen or a bedroom would be cut short by being picked up and returned to base by my mother. As soon as she wasn't looking, I was off again.

I suppose the real trouble for my parents started when I began to walk. My first vivid recollection was of the Christmas following my second birthday. We had a lovely tree decorated in our living room, and there were some interesting looking bright objects tied to it. Naturally, I wanted to get a closer look and, when I got nearer, I saw that they were sweets. I have always had a sweet tooth, and that tree full of goodies was too much to resist. Reaching up to try and spirit one away, I found that it was tied fast to one of the branches. I had more willpower than commonsense, so I tugged at the offending sweet. Still it would not budge, so I tugged harder. It was beginning to give way – but so was the tree. In what seemed like a slow motion movie, that huge green structure swayed and then toppled onto me. I let out a tiny scream of surprise, but kept clutching to that sweet. I was completely drowned in all the greenery. The next thing I remember was my mother and father groping through the branches to pull me out. My mother seemed most angry, I am sure because she was worried that I may have hurt myself, but my father was laughing when he picked me up. His laughter became even louder when he saw that I had come away with the sweet and a section of the branch grasped firmly in my hand. I've managed to get to the sweets without pulling down any more Christmas trees since then.

I love both of my parents very much, and have also spent many happy hours playing with my little brother. I have been lucky in that respect. I can remember the first time I saw Adrian most vividly. Mother came back from the hospital and I was waiting impatiently to greet her. As soon as they were in the hall, I wanted to see what was making such a protesting noise wrapped in those soft, white blankets. The baby was crying loudly, but mother handed me the bundle while father beamed proudly in the background. As soon as Adrian was in my arms he stopped crying and went happily to sleep. I was so happy – now that I knew I had a brother.

I think it often happens that the father of the family favors the daughter, and the mother the son. It was like that with us. I was six when Adrian was born, but Gheorghe, my father, when talking earlier about his wish for a son was often told by mother that he already had one – me. I certainly was not my mother's idea of the perfect daughter. I was a true tomboy.

When I was old enough to go to kindergarten my parents breathed a sigh of relief, hoping that I would work off some of my enormous energy. Unfortunately for them the opposite happened. I discovered all sorts of exciting new ideas and things to do, as well as making a host of new friends. We start our kindergarten at the age of three and I could hardly wait for the beginning of the first term. It was like a new adventure and I was itching to see what life outside my home and our apartment building was all about.

I am often asked which of my parents I most take after, which is always a difficult question to answer. People who know us have always said that, facially, I most closely resemble my father. Nowadays I can see what they mean, for as I grew older, the likeness became more apparent. From my mother, I have inherited the intensity of her eyes. I've often been criticized for what is described as a staring look in my eyes, though it never seems to trouble the children I work with – it is only adults that feel nervous or uncomfortable in my presence. It has never been something that I have been conscious of; I suppose it is just an unfortunate expression that comes with intense concentration.

I have not yet inherited my mother's enjoyment of knitting, but Adrian and I have certainly adopted our father's *joie de vivre*. My recent love, while traveling abroad, of hitting the occasional night-spot is a gentle expression of this.

Onesti is a very modern town, everything is new; the houses, shops, roads and schools – even the people are mostly young. It was a new industrial town. We lived in the center and were surrounded by boulevards and floral displays. There were very few cars or trucks to trouble us in our neighborhood so the streets were a natural playground for all the children. Everything was near by, for the cinema and the stores were right next to us, so my mother could send me to buy something without any worries. Father was out during the day at his job as a motor mechanic. He spent most of his time dealing with the huge forestry tractors and machinery. Until Adrian was old enough to go to school, mother stayed at home to keep a watchful eye on us.

We had a first floor apartment in the building, and everybody knew everybody. It was a friendly place ringing with the excited shouts of the many children playing outside or in the corridors between the concrete stairways. And then I went to kindergarten which, although it was only about three minutes walk away, seemed much further.

How I enjoyed the new experience! We spent the time playing games either in the classroom when the weather was bad, or more usually in the school playground. The rest of the time was spent in listening to marvelous tales and stories, which let our imaginations run wild. I enjoyed mucking around in the playground most of all and was a real little monster. My two favorite pastimes were turning cartwheels or doing anything vaguely acrobatic, and playing soccer with the boys. I preferred to play games with the boys rather than the girls because they were smarter and more sincere – if I could prove that I was as good as them – if not better – I could join in. At first, when I was very tiny they just laughed when I asked to play soccer, but they soon changed their attitudes. I used to practise secretly until I knew that I could give them a run for their money. I often ended up as leader of the groups that I was in but I always knew my place. In Romania, we say 'if only you could see the size of your nose' when we want to stop someone from getting too big-headed. I was mad about any physical activity, and outside school, if I was not playing soccer, I could usually be found either up a tree or swinging from one. Little did I, or anyone else, quite realize where this early athleticism would lead.

As I mentioned, Onesti was a very young town and one of its best features was the trees that were planted along all the main streets and which grew naturally in great numbers elsewhere. It meant that I had lots of raw material to practise on. Mind you, it was on the frequent visits to my grandparents that I really perfected my tree climbing. I loved going to see them. They were my mother's parents, called Ion and Iliana Blanaru, and they lived across the River Trotus some five minutes from home. It was like another world to me. I felt very much at ease over there. The countryside has always had a good effect on me; I have always loved it. A day alone in the country is the perfect cure for the problems and pressures of training.

In my grandparents' garden and throughout their area there were masses of fruit trees; in spring the blossoms were beautiful and fragrant. But autumn was always the best season for climbing, for by that time the fruit was ready for eating. Strangely, I never seemed to get stuck in trees, though I did tend to fall out of them. I never seriously hurt myself.

I remember one day when, after I had spent the entire afternoon perched at the top of a plum tree, my exasperated grandmother, having tried to coax me down with some home-made cookies, called up to me, 'Nadia, why on earth do you spend all your time climbing trees!' 'Because they're here to be climbed', I answered. 'Well why stay up there when it's more comfortable indoors or on the grass? What are you doing!' 'Just watching everything. I don't know why I like trees so much. I just do.' She looked at me long and hard and then with a strange smile turned towards the house. I heard her saying, 'She's a strange little thing.' It had never occurred to me before that I needed a reason for climbing, I simply did it because I enjoyed it. I remember those days now as a useful introduction to the problems of the asymmetric bars; after all, a swing around a bough is no different to one on the bars. It was going a bit far when on one occasion a boy had seen me jumping from a tree and shouted across the yard, 'Hey, Comaneci, want some twigs to build your nest with?'

One of the nice things about living in Onesti was that nearly all my relatives lived close by. There was always somewhere to pop across to and have a chat or a game, and hopefully a bit to eat. Two of my favorite cousins were Cristian and Sorin Pirvu and I used to spend a lot of time playing over at their place. I never had close friends, largely because I never felt the need or desire for them. With such a happy home, friendly relatives, and lots of people to play with, my life was full enough.

Towards the end of my time in the kindergarten, play-time began to take on a new significance. We were taught an elementary form of gymnastics, by Mr. Duncan who "coached" me for the first two years of my involvement in this exciting new activity.

I loved being able to run around, cartwheel, jump and swing on various objects. We all waited impatiently for the gym-classes to come around each week, and although Mr. Duncan was a teacher and had to be respected, these sessions were lighthearted periods of juvenile anarchy. We had the run of the place, but if the coach told us to stop, we stopped immediately. It opened up a whole new world for me, though at the time and for several years after, I could never have dreamed where it would eventually take me.

3

AT THE time when I was still creating havoc at the kindergarten, a gymnastics team called 'The Flame' was being formed at the Onesti Sports Club. One of its founding members was an 8-year-old girl from Comanesti called Anca Grigoras. It is a strange coincidence that the girl who I was in awe of all those years ago, has ended up being my best friend.

A Scorpio like me, Anca is blonde and blue-eyed, pretty blunt in her opinions but trustworthy and a loyal confidante. Anca is a top-class gymnast, having won a silver at Montreal, and has been one of the most consistent and respected members of the Romanian team. I have always tended to prefer the company of slightly older people and, I suppose, Anca looks at me as a kind of kid sister.

Although I became much more aware of gymnastics during the last year or so of my kindergarten, it was never something that I took seriously. It meant a lot to me because it was more physically demanding than the simpler sports, but I did not think of it as anything more than a different kind of playing and great fun. This was the kind of response that coaches looked for from all their children and for several good reasons.

In Romania, we feel that sport is very important to the healthy development of young people. From an early age teachers try to encourage an interest in it through play. This not only teaches children how to move well, it also gives them a sense of 'team spirit' and personal achievement. In this way, a child will learn how to cope with a challenge without throwing his weight around.

In gymnastics this casual method of introducing the sport to a child serves two purposes. First, at such an early age, a child is simply not afraid of the apparatus and will happily do things, on the beam for instance, that an older child might be wary of. This helps progress and is perfectly safe because the coaches are all highly qualified. Secondly, the teachers can keep a watchful eye on their pupils to see which child has a talent for what, so that eventually they can be given the chance to specialize. This was what happened to me, although at the time I was blissfully unaware of what was going on.

Although I still loved soccer and swimming, I began to get greater and greater pleasure from gymnastics. From 1967, I was training at the Onesti Sports Club and could devote more time to my one interest. All I wanted was to be as good as the members of The Flame. By this time, I was training under a Mr Munteanu who was an excellent coach. Technically brilliant with a perfect understanding of the movements of the sport, he laid the foundations upon which Bela and Marta were then able to build. By now we were all being given ballet training, initially (while I was with my kindergarten teacher, Mr Duncan) by Mili Simionescu and then later when I joined Mr Munteanu, by Marta Karoly.

One of the best things about those earlier days of gymnastics was the system that was used to hold our concentration. It always worked, keeping us keen even through some of the more boring and routine exercises. At the end of our first session, we all lined up ready to be dismissed from the class but I could not see Mr Duncan. I turned to Georgeta Gabor who was next to me, and asked, 'Where's the Professor, why isn't he here to let us go? Have we done something wrong?' She giggled and whispered, 'No, he'll be back in a second, but he'll be hiding something behind his back. Just watch and see.' She seemed to know what was going on, which made me even more curious.

Sure enough, moments later he returned with his hands firmly behind his back and looking very serious while we stood stiffly to attention. 'All right then, who thinks they did well today?' he asked sternly. We all put up our hands and he peered closely at each of us in the line. Then, with a sudden smile, he said, 'I agree. Put your hands out. I've a little reward for you.' From behind his back, he produced a small paper bag full of chocolates and as he passed, he handed one out to each of us. This ritual was followed with discretion, as I found out after fooling around in one of the lessons. If we weren't up to scratch, no chocolate; it was as simple as that. And foolproof. I have been crazy about chocolate ever since – especially white chocolate!

I am sure mother and father were hoping that with all the energy I was using up in the gymnasium, I would be less of a tearaway outside. They hid their disappointment very well. Another thing which disturbed my mother most of all, was that I didn't seem to show my affection enough and instead became ever more free-spirited and independent. I didn't realize it at the time – it was simply natural for me to be like that – but looking back on it now, I can see how my parents must have mistaken my manner for coldness. I have always been very self-contained, undemonstrative and content to show my feelings only when I felt it was absolutely necessary. A gymnast must always be controlled, during training and, even more importantly, during a performance. The sport demands total concentration, and a gymnast gets used to the idea that any extraneous expression or thought is a waste of energy.

Now I can see that, at home, there must have been many occasions when my parents would have liked me to show more warmth. My independent nature made me rather thoughtless at times. I suppose one of the best examples of this happened when I was about six. It was not a schoolday – I think it was a Sunday – and the weather was fantastic. One of my school friends had arranged to meet me that morning to go out to play at eight o'clock. She arrived on time and off we went. We decided to go to the patisserie to buy some small cakes, and then head for the woods near the edge of Onesti. We ended up window-shopping first, staring at the huge displays, imagining what we would buy if we had the money. I remember falling for some beautiful lengths of white silk ribbon that would have looked just right in my hair at the gymnastics classes. The smell of fresh baking wafting around the corner of Republicii Boulevard finally pulled us away. It did not take very long to decide which pastries we should spend our pocket-money on, and very soon we were making off for our hide-out in the woods, each of us clutching a warm bag in our hands. Although there was really nothing special about "our" place, we knew we could always go there, have little feasts, swap gossip and fairy tales, and no one would find us.

We sat and talked about gym, the teachers and the school lessons and about the big new Gymnastics Hall that was being built. We went searching for new flowers or any that were particularly colorful. We played hide-and-seek for much of the afternoon, which I was pretty good at! The sun went on shining, the birds went on singing, and the day seemed never to end. It was only when our stomachs started to rumble, that we finally went off home. It had been a glorious day.

I was surprised to find the door to our apartment open and could half hear my parents in a worried discussion. I slipped off my shoes, put them in my room, and then made a bee-line for the kitchen, calling out to my parents as I did so to let them know I was home. Their conversation stopped immediately and my father shouted, 'Nadia' in a voice that was a mixture of surprise and relief. My mother rushed into the kitchen and, taking me by the arms, shook me. 'Where on earth have you been? Why are you so late, don't you realize that it is past nine o'clock? We have been out of our minds with worry.'

I had no idea that it was so late. Even so, I could not see why they were so upset – I had been out in the evenings before now and they had never objected. It had never occurred to me that they needed to know about my plans and anyway, I had not known of them myself when I left that morning!

Their anger turned to relief. Soon I was sitting at the table eating a late snack, while my father gave me a solemn lecture about letting them know if I wanted to spend so much time away, and making sure that I got back earlier in future. I was ashamed of my thoughtlessness and deeply sorry at their distress. I did not want to hurt my parents, and even though I never quite understood why they had been so worried, I made sure never to disappear for a whole day again without giving them some idea of my plans.

I have never cried when being disciplined, either in the gym, or at school, or even at home. I suppose I must have cried as a baby, but it has not happened often since then. That is not to say that I haven't felt like it – it's just that I bottle it up. I turn all my strong feelings inwards, which, as any psychologist would tell you, is a certain recipe for disaster unless there is some means of release. Fortunately for me, there is.

Gymnastics is my emotional safety valve. If there is something that is particularly bugging me, I can work it out of my system through physical exercise that usually takes the form of gymnastics but can equally be a brisk swim, a game of tennis, skiing, or whatever's going.

My introversion is not something that I consciously developed – it was always a part of my nature, and as I got older, I put it to good use, especially in training. Anger, for whatever reason, is an easy emotion to channel into violent activity. Very often, it can be destructive, but in my case, the opposite is true. My coaches have come to recognize this in recent years. If I fail to live up to my own standards, especially in training, I get furious with myself and work twice as hard to compensate. So long as I am not injured in any way it is an approach that makes sense.

Take the Moscow Olympics, for example. After my unnecessary fall from the asymmetric bars I was so angry and disappointed that when I came to do the same exercise in Competition II, I was awarded the maximum mark from the judges. I knew then that I had done myself justice and wiped out the earlier disgrace. When I was younger, this was certainly one of the reasons why I was so quick to learn.

I started school when I was six and a half years old, in 1968. (Interestingly, the Gymnastics Hall was inaugurated February 5 of the same year, and on February 9, Bela first came to Gheorghe

Gheorghiu-Dej). In the first class I spent much of my time just getting to grips with all the strange new subjects. Sadly at this age, I was far more interested in sports than academic subjects, although this changed later when I discovered how enjoyable learning could be. I loved reading and losing myself in fascinating and grotesque stories. Chemistry was also magical: watching powders changing into liquids and strange substances taking on completely different forms. It was a year of gradual academic achievement, and at the same time my gymnastics was coming along well. So well, that by the end of the school year I was accepted at the new Gymnastics High School, which opened in September 1969. This was the best news I could have dreamed of; now I really was on my way.

The school, the hostel for the boarders, and the gymnasium were all in the same complex which made life very easy. It was only a ten minute walk from home: it all seemed too good to be true. We were spending four hours a day in the gymnasium and about four and a half in the classrooms.

I had to settle into an ordered routine which led to certain changes in my way of living. I found that I had a lot less free time because on top of the extra hours spent in the gym, I had homework to do. How I loathed that! Also, my meals were now being carefully regulated and I had to take lunch and my evening meal with the other students who lived in the hostel. This was so my intake could be accurately monitored and changed according to the demands of my training schedules. The only meal I ate regularly in the company of my family was *mic-dejun* which means breakfast.

The lessons for all subjects were structured around our gymnastics programs and this was an important factor in the success of all the groups. I really admire competitors who do not enjoy the benefits of a government prepared to help sports people. These gymnasts fight their way to the big internationals and really earn their place there because they receive the barest minimum of aid from educational authorities or their places of work. Generally, they have to train in unsociable hours, which means that they are not at their best either physically or mentally.

Our gym lesson was from eight to twelve o'clock in the morning for six days of the week, with academic lessons during the afternoon. Sometimes we would have additional coaching in the gym in the early evening, especially if there was a competition coming up. Although I was finding something strangely fulfilling in my training, I still did not take the sport too seriously, even after joining the High School. I took it to be something close to a form of structured play. I found that I was at

35

my happiest when left to myself. I knew almost instinctively what I should do, and how it could safely be done without calling the coach over to help. Marta Karoly was the head coach, with Bela, her husband assisting her. We had a marvelous staff to look after us, with doctors, physiotherapists, nutritionists, choreographers, musicians, and of course, a large number of coaches. This was, after all, the main center for our sport in Romania and it was obvious that Mili Simionescu, who had played a large part in getting the project off the ground, had thought of everything. The classroom teachers were always flexible and would make allowances for us, both during training and after competitions, when we were still recovering. One of the best things about every competition was being let off homework.

Living under such strict discipline for five and a half days of the week, it was inevitable, I suppose, that we would make up for it on our one full day off. It was great just to laze around in bed for an extra hour, and not to have to rush to get to class in time for the next lesson. There was always a game of soccer in progress somewhere near by, which meant I'd be there hoping to be asked to join in. I used to get bruised all the time, but it never worried me. I gave as good as I got, so I couldn't complain! It was just part of the game. It used to annoy me if one of the boys started crying after being accidentally kicked, 'What a cissy,' I would think. 'Boys are supposed to be tougher than girls, but you never see me cry.' I think I was rather intolerant of other people's weaknesses, especially if they were the same age as me.

However, during that first year, when I was eight years old something happened that was to change my sporting life greatly. In June 1970, the Romanian National Championships for Gymnastics were held in Sibiu. I was chosen for the competition and was due to leave on the 25th. It was very exhilarating, and there was lots of extra coaching in the weeks prior to our departure. I enjoyed the training, but without the same dedication that some of the older and much more serious members of the team were showing, like Liliana Branisteanu, who was the best of the gymnasts in our party. We all worked together in preparation for Sibiu and under Marta's expert guidance and with Bela's support our team felt more and more confident as the time approached. Before we knew it, the big day had arrived.

4

THE 1970 National Championships were to be a test case for the coaching system developed in Onesti. Marta and Bela now believed that we were ready to make our presence felt, and left us in no doubt that they expected great things of us. I suppose they were under a lot of pressure to justify the favor shown to us by the Romanian Gymnastics Federation when they gave us the use of the prestigious new center in Onesti. That explained their nervousness just before the first event when they seemed unable to stand still for more than five seconds at a time.

The competition was very close between ourselves and the team from Oradea, who were more established gymnasts than we were. Other teams did not really get a look in for the team medals. We were down to the final piece of apparatus – the beam – and the gold was still in the balance, with less than one full point separating our two teams.

My exercise followed those of my teammates, Viorica Dumitru and Liliana Branisteanu, and Liliana had earned a score of 9·00. That was going to be difficult to beat. Marta was the beam coach and before I mounted the dreaded piece of wood, she said sternly, 'Right then, get up there and show them what I've taught you. Remember the success of the team is riding on your shoulders. Concentrate, and don't let me down!' As she said this, she pushed me gently towards the podium. I knew my routine back to front – I'd been practicing it often enough in the gym over the last week or two. Having performed it so often, I was more worried about my ability to keep my enthusiasm for the exercise going than about my ability to do it. When you are that young, it is difficult to concentrate if you are not really enjoying youself.

Anyway, I mounted the beam and began my final appearance in the competition. Everything was going very smoothly. I attempted a high leap and promptly fell off the left side of the beam. Feeling angry, and very embarrassed, I re-mounted and immediately fell off on the opposite side. I could hear howls of laughter from my teammates and some of the other competitors who were sitting and watching. Funnily enough the audience was very quiet; I think the people must have been worried that I'd hurt myself. For the third time, I climbed on that damned apparatus, my ears burning. I'd been shaken out of my complacency, and was determined not to fall again. But I did! And with less than a second of my routine left to go! I clambered back up and managed to complete the correct dismount. At least this landing was solid. The next thing I remember was an almighty blow across the back of my head, delivered from a fuming Marta. What she didn't know was that I was angry enough with myself for both of us! Many other girls might have cried at this point. I knew that it would never happen again. Already, my rage was turning to resolve.

I stomped back to our team position, with Marta still snapping at me and, somewhat shamefaced, prepared to meet with Bela's anger. To my surprise, he was smiling, though not at me. He had realized that with my score of 7·25, our team had won the National Championships. It was a cause for great celebration when we returned to Onesti, but my heart wasn't in it. I still felt miserable about my awful performance on the beam and even thoughts of my earlier, good work couldn't blot that out.

I hardly noticed the official announcement of the result. We had scored 176·35 points, while Oradea had 176·25. It was one of the narrowest victories in the Championship's history. Liliana had come first in the Overall category with 37·05 points and I had come thirteenth with a score of 34·65. As far as I was concerned, the whole thing had been a nightmare. My mother and father kept telling me that I had played a vital part in a team effort but they couldn't console me.

On the night of our return to Sibiu, I sat alone in my room and brooded. I told myself that I was never going to be humiliated in such a way again, and that in future I would take my sport very seriously. I realized that I felt jealous of the winner, that I wanted so badly to trade places with her, and I knew that if I applied myself more fully to my training, I would find that first place very soon. I believed in my own ability and had great faith in my coaches, especially Bela. I suppose that this is a good time to talk about Bela and also others who helped me after my vow to take the sport more seriously. People associate my career with Bela, and even though he was not my first coach, he greatly influenced my gymnastics in those early days.

Bela and Marta Karoly are a formidable husband and wife team. They are of Hungarian extraction, rather than Romanian, as is their close colleague, Geza Poszar, the choreographer, and they would often chat amongst themselves in Hungarian. Some of the girls, like Emilia Eberle, spoke the language so there was an odd mixture of oaths in some of our training sessions! Although Marta had a background in gymnastics, Bela did not. He is a giant of a man and had experience in four sports: athletics, handball, boxing and rugby. His aim was to bring different aspects of each of these sports to a new way of coaching gymnastics; the all round strength of the athlete, the aggression of the handball player, the boxer's tough approach to suffering and the team spirit of the rugby player. You need only look at our team's beginning; he learned more from her than he had ever done at the Institute For Physical Education and Sport.

At first it was great fun having Bela with us in training, because he was learning just as much as us. While Marta's coaching was more conventional, our early sessions with Bela were pretty relaxed. His strength and size made him invaluable as a "spotter"; that is, the guy on hand to prevent any harm coming to a gymnast trying a risky dismount, or jump. If someone can catch you and hold you in mid-air, you soon learn to trust him, and out of trust grows respect. It is this combination of trust and respect that is vital to a successful partnership.

Ballet is an important part of any gymnast's training. It is one of the areas that is badly neglected in many of the Western gym clubs – and it shows. It is crucial to both the fledgling gymnast and the experienced competitor, a marvelous way of keeping the body fit and supple and, at the same time, developing artistic awareness. Geza Poszar took us for this part of our training but worked with the other coaches on every part of the program to give it continuity and grace.

As Bela's confidence grew, he made his presence felt more and more, and began to supervise the time we spent outside training hours. This was fine by me because, outside of my schoolwork, I wanted to devote more of my time to my sport. If I was not playing soccer or cycling, I would probably be in the gymnasium. In fact, as Bela's demands on our time grew, I found myself staying at the school hostel instead of going home, especially after a competition when I'd have a dose of physiotherapy to endure and often homework to finish. My family lived near by, so I did not miss them too much and by this time, my former team mate and friend, Teodora Ungureanu, had joined the school. We spent a lot of time together, and developed a healthy rivalry.

One of the changes that we noticed in Bela's approach to us was that he became very strict. Marta had always been firm with us, but Bela was much more intimidating. He demanded absolute obedience, and had complete power over us. This did not worry me too much because I was not naturally troublesome. He was a stickler for punctuality, and Teodora fell foul of this more than once.

In fact, one day when she turned up to train five minutes late, his punishment had her in tears for a couple of days. Teodora was often a few minutes late and was always being told off for chatting in our gym periods but this time Bela decided to make an example of her. We were scheduled to make our first visit outside Eastern Europe to Italy in June 1973. Teodora was included in the team but Bela told her that because she could not behave herself, she must stay behind. 'Only those of exemplary behavior and great dedication earn the chance to travel overseas and represent their country. If you can't be bothered to turn up for training on time, I am not going to be bothered to take you with me! Do you think that you deserve to go?' Teodora could say nothing, and just looked tearfully at the dark, padded floor of the hall .

Any school needs that kind of discipline, especially one full of gymnasts in their early teens. However, he did rather overdo it when we were traveling overseas. I can understand the desire of the team coach to keep his charges under a tight rein just before, and during, a competition. But I don't see why this should go on after it is all over. Maybe Bela was just being over protective, or felt he had to guard his protegées – it was probably a bit of both, but it meant that we missed out on a lot of fun. Still, I'd have wanted the extra control in my training sessions anyway, especially leading up to the 1976 Montreal Olympics and the 1977 Prague European Championships. As a team, it made us unbeatable.

Outside the gymnasium, and away from training, Bela was a changed person, as was Marta. When we went to the mountains to ski in winter or to the Black Sea resort of Mangalia in the summer, the whole atmosphere was much more relaxed and natural. He and I had some great swimming races during those vacations! Mind you, he still made us do some training, normally in the form of a two mile run each day. Bela was also a very fine hunter, and often, when he had shot some game, we would all share in a feast. Sometimes Bela would smoke the meat and then some time later he would give us some to eat for a treat after a good result, or maybe for a birthday celebration. On one of our many visits to England, Bela told one of the officials at the 'Champions All' event in London that he would love to have a fox hound and to his great delight, he was presented with one! Bela's idea of a perfect evening is to sit back with a large cognac and tell hunting stories.

Things continued to work well between Bela and myself until mid '77 when signs of strain began to show. I was nearly sixteen and had been through one of the most hectic and demanding years of my life.

Montreal and all its after-effects – especially the constant attention of the media – had left me exhausted. I was now old enough to make my own decisions about what I should be doing with my life, and started to grow more independent and assertive. Bela, Marta, and I have one great thing in common – we all have very strong wills! While I was the unquestioning pupil all went well, because I used up all my willpower on my sport, but as soon as I wanted to branch out as an individual, we were in for a stormy ride. Add to this the physical problems of growing up – the changes in height and weight and so on – and it was no surprise that my sport suffered. The clashes between Bela and myself became more frequent, and our differences more pronounced. Eventually the Federation decided that the best thing to do was to grant a "trial separation" for an undetermined period.

Officially, the reason for our splitting up was to enable Bela and Marta to take up a new position as talent scouts, searching out promising young gymnasts to train at the new center in Deva. I left for Bucharest, our capital, and started training in the 23rd August Sports Park. I was coached by Gheorghe Condovici, Iosif Hidi and Atanasia Albu. Although we all worked very hard, the atmosphere was much more relaxed. With me in the squad were friends from Onesti like Teodora, Marilena Neacsu, Dana, Cristina Itu, as well as some new faces.

The World Championships were held in Strasbourg at the end of 1978; at the last moment I had rejoined Bela. I lost a lot of weight during that competition, which is a sure sign of being unfit, and just shows how ill-prepared I was for the event. Although I picked up a gold and a silver medal, the press wrote me off as "past it". Generally, I was going through a difficult time, and the lack of any improvement in my gymnastics made me try the old partnership again, and go to study in Deva with the Karolys.

The timing was right, for by then my body had adjusted to its new shape and I started to make progress once again. Despite the odd nagging injury, the year of 1979 started well and I even managed to win the European Cup for the third consecutive time. This was followed by a success in the World Cup in Tokyo. To the outsider, all might have seemed to be going well, but this was not quite true, as the old frictions, due to our clash of temperaments, were creeping back into our relationship.

Even so, these were forgotten as we trained for the forthcoming World Championships in Fort Worth, Texas, which were also the Olympic qualifiers. There was too much at stake. Bela was very pleased with some of his squad members and saw the key to the future of

41

Romanian gymnastics in his method of training. It certainly did work very well with the youngsters, although he and Marta completely dominated them.

The year was to end on a very bitter note. I had rebelled against the heavy-handed isolation forced on us wherever we went, by retreating back inside myself, as I had been before my time in Bucharest. I obeyed Bela to the "T", trusted no one from outside our tiny group and ceased to communicate with the outside world. Once again, all my statements were directed through him. I felt like a marionette. We had a tour en route to the games at Fort Worth. After leaving England, we had to go to Mexico. It was there that I picked up a particularly vicious stomach bug. This was about one week before the World Championships were to start. I was around 48 kilos when I went to Mexico City, but by the time I reached Fort Worth, I weighed a mere 42 kilos. I felt terribly weak and, despite massive doses of vitamins, completely run down. I knew that there was no way that I could compete.

My duty to the team was spelled out in no uncertain terms; I was to make an appearance in the arena which was all that was really necessary to be sure that the team qualified for the Team Finals. I looked as terrible as I felt, which was pretty bad.

And there was another problem besides my general weakness, for a small sore on my wrist, caused after I scratched myself with the buckle on a pair of handguards, was now inflamed. It became badly infected, and my body was simply not strong enough to resist. Having done the necessary for the team, I was whisked away to a hospital because it had been decided that an operation was urgently required.

The press had a field day. I don't deny that my bad physical condition was news and that there was obviously a story behind it, but it would not have been too difficult to find out the true reasons for my ill health during those championships, or at least, it should not have been. This is one area where Bela and some of the senior team officials don't help their own cause – they just will not talk about many of the things that most interest the press, which makes it all too easy for misconceptions to grow up about us.

I was in a hospital in Dallas for four days, and the treatment I received was excellent. All the staff were very kind and sympathetic. Although a hospital is hardly the most pleasant place to be, I was at last able to relax. Nicolae Vieru, the Secretary General of our Federation, and Bela came to visit me frequently, and the nurses and doctors brought me in lots of magazines to read. The operation has left me with a two inch scar on my left wrist. One lovely postscript to my stay in the hospital was that when I was back in Deva, two of the American doctors telephoned me just to give me their best wishes and check that everything had cleared up. I was really touched by that.

One of the less pleasant things that I managed to do while in hospital was to read the local press reports about both myself and the competition. Although our team had beaten its old enemy, the Russians, the press was less interested in our victory than in criticizing the Romanian "system" for producing "stunted and starved teenagers".

In the *Dallas Morning News* I read that I was '. . . a stunning sight, at once triumphant and tragic . . . movements now are unladylike . . . more power than grace.' What could I do about it? I was not permitted to say anything – that was left to our officials, and, more often than not, they refused to comment on such stories. The press' speculation about drugs, hypnosis, over dieting and the like was allowed to go unchecked.

5

AS I am sure you have gathered, I have grown to become a bit suspicious of the press. More than that though, I am nervous of the attention of the press, or TV and radio because I find them intrusive.

In Romania I have not been bothered too much by our reporters, for they are all aware of the need to avoid interfering with my training program. The questions that they tend to ask are factual and normally relate to specific aspects of my career which their editors feel are either informative or inspirational to other young people. Fortunately, I tend to have the edge when being interviewed because the journalists are often intimidated by my reputation. I've never been one for using twenty words when two would do, so my responses to questions tend to be very brief and succinct, and accordingly, don't make the most interesting reading. The same goes for those times when a television or film crew descends on the gymnastics hall to tape an interview or produce a film profile. On the one hand I resent such intrusions into my life, on the other I have to admit that the media are largely responsible for the popularity and success of my sport.

Outside Romania, I have been disillusioned by the behavior of large sections of the press although radio and television reporters have not given me many problems. In foreign countries there is also the difficulty of having to speak through an interpreter. I only started studying English on a full time basis when I was thirteen, so my command of English was limited when I achieved my first major successes at Skien in 1975 and Montreal in 1976.

One of the first things I discovered was that reporters keep asking the same questions:

    – Do you ever get scared?
    – Was it a surprise to get a perfect mark?
    – What do you think of Olga Korbut?
    – Which of you is the best?

– How long have you been doing gymnastics?

– Why do you never smile?

– Is your training very severe?

– Do you have a boyfriend?

– What is your favorite color/food/apparatus?

At the end of the day, after going through all the mental and physical torture of a big competition, the last thing anyone wants to do is shadow-box with the world's press and TV reporters. But this is exactly what the organizers insist on, and protocol demands that I obey. I must confess to being a shy person. It may seem odd that I can be shy and very introspective, and yet participate in a sport that is expressive and demonstrative. The two are not incompatible, for, as I have said, I lose myself in my sport and it is not the private me that is seen at a competition or exhibition. It is a young gymnast seeking perfection – the only Nadia I am happy to let the public see.

My friends tell me that I am not as shy as I used to be in the early days. But at the Montreal conferences, for example, when I was fourteen and a half years old, the whole affair seemed baffling and frightening. Frightening because of the numbers of journalists and photographers who all seemed to be shouting in my direction at the same time. Baffling because they never seemed able to accept the answers that I gave them. Some of them became quite heated, and for the first time I realized that they were not looking for my genuine views but for the answers they wanted to hear. They seemed unable, or unwilling, to believe my simple replies. While I am certain that at that age I may have made some of the answers appear unusually simplistic, they were generally what I felt to be true.

For example, the question as to whether I ever felt frightened at some of the things I do in my exercises brought my reply, 'Never'. The answer is perfectly true, but the reporter who asked at the first Montreal press conference persistently refused to accept it. Why? Probably because he thought of me as being like any other fourteen year old girl, but I don't believe that any Olympic competitor is like the vast majority of other people. The reason that I am never fearful of any of my risk elements is that I know I can handle them if I concentrate properly. They are all technically possible and if the mechanics of a movement are understood and the body is capable of achieving it, what is there to fear? At the top, confidence in one's own ability is everything. Lose that and your competitive career is over.

As the years, and the changes in my life, rolled on, I became aware that many of the questions were loaded. Fortunately, my understanding of English and French improved, so I was able to fence them effectively with or without the aid of an interpreter. Mind you, on many occasions I preferred to play dumb and pretend that I could not understand what was being asked. More and more questions about my relationship with my coaches, drug abuse, politics, my private life, were being thrown at me, which prompted intervention by our team management. The reporters were often hostile and delivered their questions in such a way as to try and catch me out. By choosing to remain silent I became the target for the sensation seekers who would peddle any old story. According to popular wisdom, there was some sinister and secret reason for my silence.

The worst, and most cruel, example of the kind of wild speculation I have been the target of was the report of my "attempted suicide" which appeared in some journals in West Germany, Italy, and Great Britain. According to the first of these reports, I had drunk two bottles of disinfectant because I was heartbroken at the breakup of an affair I was supposed to have had with some forty-two your old poet. A story like that probably earned the journalist involved a small fortune and no doubt helped to boost the newspaper's circulation figures.

So where had this story come from? It certainly suggested a fertile imagination, or a remarkable access to police and hospital secret records for, if such information were true, it would hardly be public knowledge. Not even a Romanian newspaperman could have found out unless I had died, or failed and been prosecuted under Romanian law (suicide is still a crime in Romania). So where did this particular gem originate?

It seems to have been a case of someone hearing part of a story, greatly enlarging upon it and then later interpreting as tacit admission the fact that it was never denied.

The truth was that I had swallowed something that violently disagreed with me and that I had been involved in a bitter row with some officials who were with me in Bucharest. To clear up this matter for once and for all, let me first set the scene.

I was staying at the 23rd August Sports Hotel in Bucharest, where I had been promised that I would be allowed more freedom than I had been used to under Bela and Marta. The team doctor had also given me permission to take a short break from training. This would give me a chance to recover from the strain of the previous months.

The day in question was my wash day and I had some leotards, gymsocks, and underwear to deal with. I decided to pop down the corridor to borrow some bleach from one of the other girls, but when I opened our outer door I was confronted by one of the women team officials who immediately asked, 'Nadia, where are you going? Is there

47

something that you want?' Now ordinarily, that is not the sort of question that should upset anyone, but I was finding that every time I wanted to leave my room, there was somebody "casually" asking what I was up to. I suppose that they felt nervous about being responsible for me, but I felt angry because I was being denied the extra freedom I'd been promised. At least under Bela, I always knew where I stood even if I didn't like it or agree with it. Anyway, I went to get the bleach and came back with a cup full. Instead of doing my washing right away, I decided to write a letter home and, putting the cup down on the desk in the corner of the room by the window, I sat there and wrote, mentioning the crazy amount of protection which I had to put up with. The more I wrote about it, the more it made me angry. I finished the letter, discovered that I needed some stamps and went to borrow some from one of my teammates. When I opened the inner door to my room, there were three of the officials playing cards outside my room. 'Going somewhere?' came the inevitable query. I hit the roof. I could take no more.

'What the hell are you doing here? Why is it that I can't even visit the TV room without being cross-examined. I am supposed to be here to relax, get some peace and quiet. How can any one feel relaxed with you people ready to jump on me at every corner? You are driving me mad! I'd rather be back with Bela. Just leave me alone!'

I hardly registered the stunned and silent faces of the three guards. In an almost blind fury I stormed back into my room and slammed the door behind me. I threw myself into the chair by the desk and banged my letter down on the top. I was shaking with rage. I had some fruit juice in one of the cups there, and I picked it up and took a huge gulp. I wanted to calm myself. Before I realized what I had done, I felt a hideous burning sensation in my throat and stomach – I had reached for the wrong cup. I had swallowed the bleach, though not all of it, mercifully. In agony, I called out for help from the girls in the room next to mine. I had tried to make myself sick, but could not. I think it was Dana who rushed in and called immediately for a doctor. Luckily, in the 23rd August complex, we have a Sports Medicine Center, so help was very quick in arriving. Within two days, I was back on my feet as if nothing had happened.

I suppose, looking back now, my tirade was a little hard on those over-protective individuals. They had borne the brunt of three years pent up frustration. A lot of people must have heard the argument, or perhaps I should say furious monologue. When they heard about the bleach, they put two and two together and made twenty-two.

One of the girls said to me one evening when we were quietly

listening to some music, 'Be honest now, you drunk that stuff on purpose, didn't you? You wanted to make them suffer. You want to make them let you go back to the Karolys, don't you? It was all a big gesture, a cry for help, wasn't it?'

When she asked that, I felt very angry that she should think so. It was then that I realized how it must have looked. For a split second, I thought she could be right and that I had deliberately taken the bleach. But no – of course I hadn't, I didn't know what I'd drunk until I had swallowed it.

But had I done it subconsciously? Well, no one knows exactly what goes on in the back of his or her mind but I do know I never once considered committing suicide or making some grand gesture that afternoon.

The outcome of the whole incident was that I was transferred at my request, and with Bela's evident approval, to Deva. However it was not long before Bela and I were at loggerheads again.

How the story that eventually appeared became so scandalously distorted remains a mystery. Similarly, God only knows where the story on my passionate affair with the forty-two year old poet came from! Such stories have left me feeling somewhat bitter towards the press – although I suppose that I must count myself as one of them nowadays.

Let me explain: in Romania, one of our top newspapers is called *Scinteia Tineretului*, a popular youth paper rather than one which is devoted to a particular subject like economics, sport, or science. To my great surprise, I was asked by the editor to write a weekly column in response to letters sent in by readers – a form of "agony column". It has been an intriguing experience for me; I have had to go through about 700 letters a week to choose three or four to reply to. In this I am helped by Horias Alexandrescu, one of Romania's best sports writers, who does a lot of the filtering of the best letters. The majority of them are from young people who are seeking a little encouragement in their school lessons or their sport. I do occasionally get the odd abusive letter, though the writers are often too cowardly to sign their names!

What is both touching and a little frightening is the way that so many people treat me with such respect – in their eyes I have no faults.

One of the dubious pleasures of being famous, both in Romania and nowadays when I am abroad as well, is that I am not free to walk down a busy street without being either stared at or accosted. A simple shopping trip can turn into a nightmare. Even if I can get past the other shoppers, I suddenly find myself surrounded by assistants; within half an hour, an acute attack of "autographer's cramp" sets in.

Of course, there are always times when a little fame can come in handy! The phrase, 'It's for Nadia' can work wonders at speeding things up, or cutting through yards of red-tape. It's naughty, but I can't resist beating "the system" once in a while. Even when I go with a team to some obscure place in the far corners of Romania, I still find myself being troubled by people. The only time I feel really annoyed by autograph hunters is when they approach me at a dining table, as I like to take eating very seriously. I try to give little children time and attention; it's their parents that are the nuisance!

In these days of big-money and ultra-nationalistic sports, gymnasts suffer outside pressures which I feel to be in the interest of anything but the sport itself. Due to the enormous amount of national prestige at stake in major competitions, a "win at any cost" mentality has developed in those who supervise the sporting bodies. The Federations care tremendously about getting good results and they pass on that pressure to the coaches and thence to the gymnasts. I feel that national pride tends to dominate international competitions to such an extent as to be dangerous to the future of gymnastics.

It doesn't seem reasonable to put this amount of stress on the shoulders of a gymnast who has enough to worry about in the apparatus. It is doubly unfortunate that the problem is most serious in the women's competitions, because most of the girls are only in their mid-teens and are probably finding it difficult to cope with growing up. I think I am very lucky to have the sort of mentality that, when I enter the gymnastics arena, allows me to completely forget everything extraneous to my performance.

At Fort Worth, however, I could not avoid feeling pressurized by my team's determination to do well. It became clear very quickly that my previous illness had left me in no fit state to compete. I needed a long period of rest and recuperation. After the compulsory exercises in the team event, I left for All Saints Hospital for treatment on my infected wrist. I returned to the competition hall to do little more than sit it out.

However, with the Soviet team losing ground to us, it looked as though we might have a chance to beat them. And then disaster occurred, for Emilia Eberle fluffed her beam exercise. Bela could see our golden opportunity slipping away from us, and felt that there was only one thing left he could do. 'Right Nadia', he said, 'you will have to go on the beam. I know you weren't expecting to compete, but you can see the position – we can take the Russians. Just give us a good performance and, after that, the girls will hold their own. One faultless exercise is all that we need to give us the necessary edge. I know your hand is hurting a bit, but you must do it! We're depending on you.' He left me with nothing to say.

Taking off my track-suit trousers, I started to warm up in front of our team position. Every time I tried to complete a move involving hand support, the pain was awful. In gymnastics, it is necessary to be able to endure pain and rise above it. It was suddenly my turn on the beam, and receiving a rare *Noroc bune* from my teammate Melita Ruhn, (it means good luck), I stepped onto the podium. The audience became unusually quite. I began my exercise, which became more and more agonizing, and, by the end, my wrist felt as if it was on fire. A perfect dismount signalled the end, and oblivious to the crowd's appreciation I sat down and waited for the judges' verdict. 9·95 was the score, I could hardly have done more. But really I should not have risked causing permanent damage to my wrist. When I become a coach, I will never expect one of my girls to jeopardize her health in such a way.

The bias displayed by certain judges is another example of tension within the sport. This was dramatically illustrated at the 1977 European Championships in Prague, which many felt to be the most blatant example of unfair marking at a world class competition. Unfortunately I found myself smack at the center of it all. The issue was not about whether Nelli Kim or I was the better vaulter, but was all about a struggle between the two countries we had been chosen to represent.

Prague left a bitter taste in many people's mouths.

6

THE 1977 European Championships were very important to me because I was defending the title of European Champion. These competitions are held every two years, the previous one having been held in Skien, a tiny town in Norway. Although it had been my first big international, at the time I'd been too young to consider it as anything more than just another competition. Even when I was taking part I didn't realize how important an event it was.

In April 1975, just before the Europeans, I had gone to London to take part in "Champions All". I was just getting over an attack of influenza when we left for England. Bela had decided to use this competition to sharpen me up for Skien. I was excited to be visiting London, for it was one of those cities that we read a lot about in our school text books, and often see pictures of in magazines or on the TV. I knew all about Buckingham Palace, the Houses of Parliament, Tower Bridge, and Windsor Castle. At last, I was going to get the chance to see them for myself.

On the flight over to London, Bela was by my side making sure that I was in the right frame of mind for the task ahead.

'When we get to the hotel, I want you to go to bed as early as possible. We must be certain that you fully recover from your flu. Tomorrow we'll be able to try out the apparatus, but it will be in front of the press. Don't worry, just ignore them. Simply do what we have been doing all the time in training. If you do that, I know we'll win. Just remember everything I have taught you.'

I nodded in silent agreement, for I knew what he said was true, – and above all else, I wanted very much to win. Maria Simionescu – Mili – travelled with us, for she was judging, and went to great trouble to make sure that everything was done to make me as comfortable as possible. I was being made quite a fuss of, and I enjoyed it, but there was the more serious business of the competition to concentrate on.

It all went as Bela had planned and I found myself standing on the victory rostrum clasping a bouquet which was almost bigger than me. I could not work out who had the biggest smile, Bela or Mili. I felt a little bemused by all the attention of the journalists and photographers. I particularly remember Avril Lennox, the British Champion at that time; she was very sweet to me while I was there and gave me some little gifts. The audience was friendly and encouraging.

One of the things I like best about competitions in London is the opportunity to go shopping around Oxford Street. I'll always remember that on my first trip in 1975, I bought a skirt for forty pence. That's what I call value for money!

However, no sooner was "Champions All" over, than Bela was turning my attention towards the European Championships in Skien. They were only three weeks away and there was still much to do. My winning score in London would not be enough to guarantee me a victory in Skien, as I only got 37·30 out of a maximum of 40. Bela, Marta, Geza, Stabisevschi (our pianist), and I spent every last minute in the training hall.

And so, at the beginning of May, we arrived in Skien, a small town of about 30,000 inhabitants known primarily as the birthplace of Ibsen, and Heavy Water.

The hall had a strangely subdued atmosphere, which I think was largely due to the strip lighting. I found it rather pleasant, almost restful. Bela was delighted to be able to re-open the sporting rivalry with Tourischeva and Kim. I had met them both before, and looked forward to competing against such tough opposition.

My first meeting with Nelli Kim had been in the German Democratic Republic, in the Friendship Cup. This was on the August 24, 1973, the day after Romanian Independence Day, and it had been a very closely fought contest between the two of us. In the Overall competition, the score was 37·85 to me and 37·65 to Nelli. She was placed higher than me in the floor exercise, we were equal on the beam, and I managed to win the vault and bars.

Ludmilla Tourischeva and I had had our first meeting in Paris in 1974, which I shall go into at greater length later on. It was a remarkable debut for Teodora and myself in many ways. My victory over the great Soviet sportswoman, as Bela often reminded me, was the most important kind – a psychological one. It was a far-sighted and courageous decision by Nicolae Vieru, our Secretary General, to send such young and relatively inexperienced girls to the demonstration in Paris.

So back to Skien, in the pre-Olympic year, where there were a lot of reputations at stake. Most people thought that the competition was going to be between Tourischeva, Kim, and Zinke of the DDR. The only member of our team who came into their calculations was our senior national champion, Alina Goreac. It would have been nice to have also been competing against Olga Korbut, but she had suffered one of her frequent "ankle injuries". As I said earlier, as far as I was concerned, this was just another competition of no great personal significance.

The first exercise was the floor, in front of a packed auditorium of about 5000 spectators. The defending champion, Tourischeva, had a poor start. At the previous championships she had taken every gold medal, but this was not her lucky day. The first event was to decide the overall winner, with the individual apparatus finals on the following day, May 4. Bela was unmoved by my floor mark of 9·65, but that day he radiated confidence, and my next discipline was the vault. 'OK, now show them what a Tsukahara should look like. I want plenty of elevation. Just imagine you are in the gym back home. Don't get too high on to the horse. Right, off you go!' And off I went, receiving 9·7 for my effort. Next came the bars, my favorite apparatus; I finished the exercise with my "Comaneci dismount" and the judges awarded me 9.75. I got the same for my last piece, which was the floor. At the end of the day, the medals fell this way:

1:	Nadia Comaneci	38·85
2:	Nelli Kim	38·50
3:	Annelore Zinke	37·95

Bela was on top of the world feeling that we had confounded the experts with our success. I was tired. It had been a long day, and the following day we would have to go through it all over again. I wanted to get an early night to prepare for training the next morning. I was grateful to Bela for keeping the press well away from me. I slept well that night.

Refreshed, I awoke to a light breakfast, some physiotherapy, and left to go for training. It was a normal routine which I was used to at any competition. The only thing that had changed since our visit began was that our morning session now played to a huge and completely absorbed audience. They cheered everything that we did but it didn't affect my concentration. I just got on with it. If I had not been able to work properly, I hesitate to think what Bela might have said to our audience. He can be quite formidable if he feels that his gymnasts aren't being given a proper chance.

The Individual Apparatus Finals began in the early evening, and things went fairly well. I picked up the gold medals for the bars, beam, and vault, but had to be content with the silver for the floor behind Nelli

Kim. My teammates were elated at the result. I was reasonably satisfied, but I would have liked to have equalled Tourischeva's clean sweep of medals in 1973.

I was happy to be leaving for home as I had missed my family very much. I still did not realize just what we had achieved in Norway, and it was only when we arrived at Bucharest Otopeni Airport that it was brought home to me. We were confronted by huge cheering crowds, and I was greeted by my mother, weeping tears of joy. Although I was surprised by the enthusiasm of the crowds in the capital, I was completely overwhelmed by my welcome when I arrived back in Onesti. Congratulations, flowers, and kisses rained down on me wherever I went. The biggest surprise of all, however, was the flood of letters we received from all over the world praising our success in the Europeans. My only regret is that I had neither the time nor the money to be able to reply to them.

So, that was how I first managed to get my hands on the European Trophy, and came to be defending it in Prague two years later. Between the two, something had happened that was to dramatically change gymnastics: the awarding of top marks to a candidate thought to have achieved perfection. That first award of 10·00 spurred gymnasts and coaches to strive for even higher levels of technical difficulty. A new breed of gymnast was emerging in the women's events. She was smaller, leaner, younger, technically superior, and more accepting of danger than her predecessors. The higher risk factor was a step forward that could never be reversed.

This development has been blamed on my approach to gymnastics. Whatever the truth, by the time of the Prague Championships in 1977, the margin for error had been so reduced that there was little hope of victory after the slightest mistake. The top five or six competitors were no more than a few tenths of a point apart.

My main rivals were the Soviet Union and East German competitors. As far as the East German team went, Steffi Kraker was going to be the biggest threat. The Soviet team was led by Nelli Kim with able support from the dimunitive Maria Filatova. There was a new name in their line up who had caught my attention in training, Elena Mukhina. I was very curious to see her, having heard her described as a Russian version of myself by an English commentator. She certainly proved to be my closest rival at Prague and came to be my greatest threat over the next year or so. Nobody could have predicted the tragedy that occurred just before the Moscow Olympics. Sadly, the chance of serious injury has grown with the increase in the degree of risk in gymnastics. Elena's broken neck was a terrible lesson to us all.

56

Elena was in the national squad, and in preparation for the Games, undergoing some intensive training. She had recently been somewhat off form and was working doubly hard to insure her place at least as first reserve for the Olympic Team. The accident occurred in her floor exercise at the end of one of the tumbling sequences, and it was the sort of thing that could happen to any of us in training when we are not using crash-mats. We use them until we have perfected the moves and afterwards tend to work without them as we would have to in a major competition.

So close to the Games, Elena would have been doing something with which she was entirely familiar and had probably repeated over a hundred times. However, as one of the world's top gymnasts, she could be expected to include many elements of high risk, in order to give her a chance of acquiring the necessary bonus points. The final somersault in one of her sequences required her to land on her neck and shoulders, and then roll to a standing position. Having completed the first full *salto* successfully, something apparently went wrong in the second aerial phase and she landed heavily on her neck. It broke. She was nearly killed, suffered severe paralysis and owes her survival to the speedy and brilliant surgery of her doctors at the hospital. She has since gained some slight degree of motor control, and I hope that she continues to recover. She was a fine exponent of our sport.

At Prague, things started in an orderly manner though we expected the Soviet team to go all out to regain the Overall Individual Title it had lost at the previous Europeans and, of course, during the intervening Olympics. We were equally determined to put up a fight. We had a good chat before the first day started.

'Excuse me, sir,' asked Teodora, who was sitting with me in the hotel room, 'but what are our instructions for the competition today?'

We awaited Bela's reply: 'The standard will be very high, it's going to be tough to win, but both of you have an excellent chance if you do as you have been told. Our preparation has been going well, but your body tension is a bit slack, Teodora, and you are a little overweight at the moment.'

Teodora looked up at him with an air of injured defiance.

'Yes. I know you are having a difficult time right now,' said Bela, 'but you will have to overcome these physical problems. You must make your body do what you want and not the other way round.'

I felt sorry for Dorina, (that's what we call Teodora) because growing up causes all sorts of unwanted changes in our physical makeup, and there is little that we can do about it. It is a period that has simply to be weathered.

'As for you Nadia, I expect nothing less than complete sureness and concentration. You know what you have to do, so I want to see you go out there and do it. I will not accept failure, of any sort, for there is no excuse for it. You can win again, so long as you do as I tell you. I know you won't let me down, in fact I expect great things of all of you. Remember, everyone will be watching your every move. Don't disappoint them. Right, go to it!'

'Yes sir', we shouted in unison, standing to attention as is the custom when our coach is addressing us.

What Bela had not told us was that there were some foul moves afoot designed to block our path to victory. I don't suppose that if he *had* let us know it would have made any difference, and I doubt that we would have understood what it was all about. It was only some time afterwards that the significance of what went on behind the scenes became apparent.

The first day passed without incident, and it looked as though it would be a good, clean contest. The result in the Overall classification was:

1: Nadia Comaneci		39·30
2: Elena Mukhina (USSR)		38·95
3: Nelli Kim (USSR)		38·85

I remember little at all about that day's competition, being totally engrossed in my own performance. What pleased me at the end of that day, as much as another gold medal to take back to my country with the European Trophy for another two years, was that my score had improved since Skien. My score there would only have earned me third place two years later.

However, the day of the Apparatus finals was a sad day for our sport. Once again, it was not the gymnasts who offended the sporting code, it was the senior officials and some of the judges. The competition was very tough, and I started on the bars. If any of the first three placed gymnasts were to put a foot wrong it would cost them a medal. It was a fight between Steffi Kraker, Elena Mukhina, and myself and there was almost nothing separating us. The result was that Elena and I shared the gold with a score of 19·650 and Steffi Kraker received the bronze on 19·600 points. It was after this that the trouble started.

The next discipline was the vault and at the end of the first round, Nelli, myself, and Elena were vying for the three medals. Once again, it could hardly have been closer. Nothing less than perfection would secure the gold. I had to follow Nelli in my vault. She had opted for a complex one, and she performed it reasonably well. She made two slight mistakes, one in the post-flight phase, and the other on landing. I knew that I was in with a chance of first place. I chose a less complex vault but still carrying the maximum number of points.

What this meant was that, under the old Code of Points, both of our vaults were marked out of a total of 10 points, and that deductions would be made for deviations from the perfect version of the particular vault. Thus, if I could put in a near perfect one, I should get a higher score. There was no doubt in Bela's mind that I would do it, for all my exercises had been going well.

Interestingly, many people in Prague had suggested that all my exercises were better than those I had performed at Montreal when I'd been given the perfect marks. All I knew was that I had every reason to suppose I would do well here. After my routine on the bars, I felt more confident than ever, and having just witnessed Nelli's vault, I was sure that the only person who could deny me victory would be myself. How naive I was!

After an encouraging pat on the back from my coach, I prepared for my two vaults. Bela placed the springboard in the right position, and making sure that he was not in the judges' line of sight, he waited for my first attempt. He nodded his approval, and I returned to the start of the runway and waited for the green light. My second vault was solid – the moment I landed I knew I had succeeded. Bela was jubilant, and the crowd was roaring approval. I sat down next to Teodora after Marta had congratulated me. We all waited eagerly for the judges' confirmation and up it came: I had won the gold.

But just after the score was put up we noticed that the judges were involved in a heated discussion. The Soviet team had apparently lodged a protest to the jury of appeal. The argument centered around three of the most senior officials of the FIG, Yuri Titov, President, of the USSR, Ellen Berger, President of the Women's Technical Committee (WTC), and Mili Simionescu, First Vice President of the WTC.

Bela evidently had guessed what had happened and went across to Mili to check out what was going on. I saw him throw up his arms in despair and, shaking his head from side to side, he came back to the team position. He turned to Marta and said very simply, 'It's started. We might as well pack up and go home now, they're changing the rules in the Code as they go along! I thought we were all supposed to be sportsmen – it makes me sick!'

Marta and he exchanged words with each other in Hungarian and then turned to us. 'Never mind them, just shame them by ignoring their little games and carry on working like before. The spectators know what's fair.'

He didn't need to tell me to ignore the judges, for as he knows, that is something I have always done.

The argument between the judges and team officials continued in the arena opposite a video monitor-screen. I could not understand what the problem was, for everyone knew that mine was the better performed vault. The next thing I heard was that the marks had been changed so that Nelli and I shared first place. I thought it unfair, but it did not worry me. Still, this result did not settle the matter and the debate started up again. When the discussions eventually stopped, it was obvious that Berger, Titov, and the judges who sided with them had won the day. Mili was looking very distressed and there were several judges and senior officials who, evidently agreeing with her stand, were trying to console her.

The actual result of the vault final was a surprise to the watching world, for after the second round of discussions I found myself in the remarkable situation of having gone from first position, to first equal, finally to be downgraded to second place. The gold medal was finally hung around Nelli's neck. The final scores were:

> 1: Nelli Kim (USSR)   19·525
> 2: Nadia Comaneci (Rom)   19·500
> 3: Elena Mukhina (USSR)   19·450

When Nelli went up to receive the gold, she shrugged her shoulders apologetically, as if to say, 'Don't blame me, I had nothing to do with it'. Nobody blamed Nelli, for like us, she is only interested in her sporting performance. There was no animosity between any of us on the victory rostrum. The applause was polite rather than enthusiastic. I felt let down by those who are supposed to be the guardians of our sport but, more than that, I felt that they had let the sport down.

All that I could do was move on to the next piece of apparatus; the balance beam. Nothing of any particular interest occurred during the course of the exercise. It went very smoothly, and Bela was waiting for me as soon as I had finished. I assumed that he was there either to congratulate or criticize, but what happened next came as a complete shock.

Walking back to our team position, he said, 'OK, put your track-suit on, and pack up your kit. We are leaving.'

Dumbfounded, I obeyed, although I still had the floor exercise to come, and I wanted to see what mark I would get for the balance beam. I could see that the rest of our party was ready to leave, so, pausing just to put on some track-shoes, I picked up my bag and we all filed out of the competition hall behind Bela. A serious-faced Nicolae Vieru (our Secretary General) was waiting at the exit for us, and he gently ushered us out. Apparently, it was a while before those in the hall realized that the Romanian Team was missing.

Under the rules, as we had left without the consent of the Head Judge, we were now disqualified, and that meant I had to give my beam medal to Elena Mukhina. Therefore it went down in the record books as a victory to the USSR; they must have been delighted.

The reason for our walk-out was explained to us by Nicu on the way back to our hotel. Virtually the whole of Romania had been watching the championship and the public was evidently infuriated by the behavior of the judges involved in the dispute, as it appeared to be directed purely at our team. Our officials decided that there was little chance of fair play so, rather than let the National Team be further insulted, we were instructed to withdraw.

The whole unsavoury affair led to a major inquiry by the FIG which resulted in the Code of Points being amended; it was felt that the old Code gave judges too much room for subjective interpretation. While the new Code is undoubtedly tighter in its control, there have been some early problems.

Although it was a sad way to leave a competition, there were some unexpected bonuses. Firstly, we were pleased to be returning home to our families a little earlier than planned; that is always a pleasure. But we'd also managed to collect a large amount of chocolate while we were away and Bela had promised that we could tuck into it once the championships were over! I managed to make my share last a reasonable time; Teodora wasn't as lucky!

Still, at least I was European Champion on returning from Prague. It was another two years before the next European Championships and they would be in Brondbyhallen in Copenhagen. There, I was to take my revenge on two of the competitors who triumphed against me at the World Championships at Strasbourg in 1978, namely Natalia Shaposhnikova and Elena Mukhina. I was delighted to win the Overall title in Copenhagen for the third time in succession as well as the golds for floor and vault, and bronze on the beam. It not only made fools of most of the press who had said I was losing my form after Strasbourg, but it earned me the European Trophy outright. It was a marvelous prize to be able to keep in my possession.

In fact, by now my trophy cupboard was crammed with medals and cups that I'd won both as an individual competitor and as a Romanian team member. I feel particularly proud of the latter.

Nadia:

Her Life in Pictures

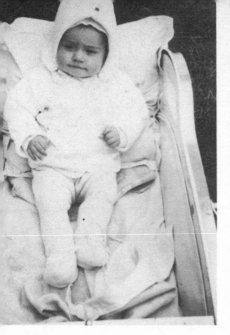

Nadia at six months

Gheorge and Stefania, Nadia's parents

Nadia (far left) on her way home from school

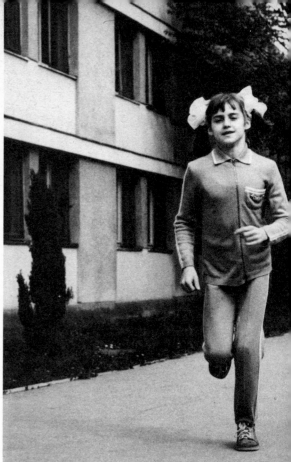

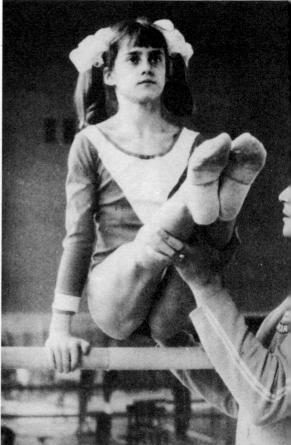

Nadia in training with
Bela Karoly her former coach

The celebrations after
the European Championships
in Skien in 1976

MONTREAL OLYMPICS, 1976

Passing through security at Montreal

Triumph at Montreal

'Little Miss Perfect'

The reception at Bucharest Airport after Montreal

Nadia, Teodora and Mariana
after a gymnastics demonstration
in Antibes, France

Nadia outside th
apartment in O

Nadia and Teodora
visit a mine in Maramures

Nadia takes General Dragnea
and Nicolae Vieru of
the Romanian Gymnastics'
Federation for a boat ride

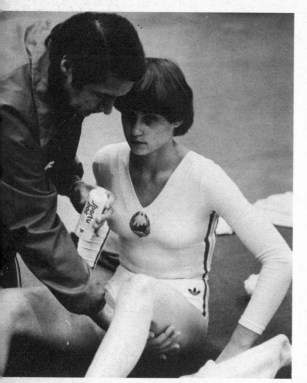

Nadia watching Emilia on the b

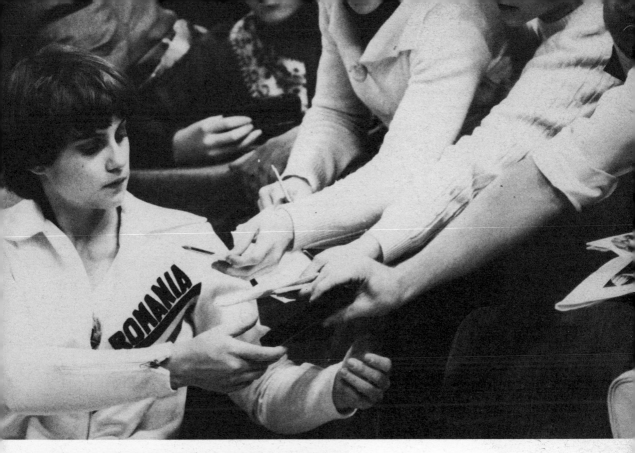

Elena Mukhina, Nadia and Emilia Eberle

Nadia, Teodora, Emilia, Gabi, Marilena, Melita, Marta Karoly and Geza Poszar

Skiing in the Carpathians

Nadia, with Cristina and Marilena (behind) in a science class at school

Nadia and Adrian in Deva

Nadia beseiged by reporters

Winter 1979 in Fort Worth, USA

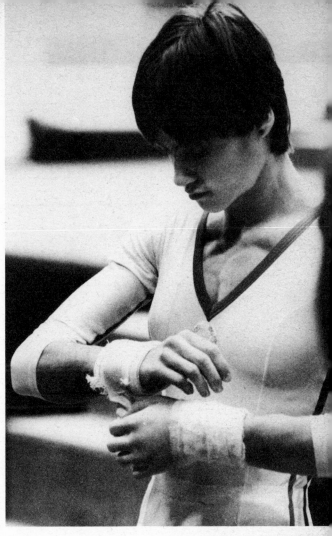

European Championships, Copenhagen 1979

On the way to another
Olympic gold, Moscow 1980

7

OUR TRIPS to health resorts during the summer and winter breaks are an essential ingredient in our training program, with the added bonus that they afford a break from the gymnasium routine and the city. In the summer, we go to a resort like Mangalia, on the Black Sea coast, which has the special treatment facilities that can help to tone us up and ease any aches and pains that accumulate over a period of five months of training, competing, and giving demonstrations. These resorts are not the exclusive preserve of sportsmen, and many of the people in the centers and hotels are overseas tourists. They are truly cosmopolitan places.

In the winter, after a spell at a spa we may go skiing for a week or so, during which we would begin light body preparations for the rigors of the season ahead. The relaxation that we are allowed on these occasions is a vital antedote to our normal lifestyle. One of the other benefits of these brief vacations is that, staying in hotels, our meals are a little more varied. Admittedly, our team doctor travels with us and keeps an eye on our diet, but nowadays, I am allowed a pretty free hand. I don't seem to have any weight problems any more and can eat almost anything without worrying. In any case, I rarely have the desire to over-indulge.

I often feel sorry for the other girls when we sit down to a meal; they might be sitting in front of a lunch consisting of yogurt, followed by a grilled chicken and fresh green vegetables, while I might tuck into soup, fillet of pork with potatoes and vegetables, perhaps finishing with some fruit and a roll and cheese.

A recent visit to Baile Felix in winter, to recharge our batteries, can be taken as a good example of a typical visit to one of these spas. The group consisted of Gheorghe, our coach, and his wife and children, our doctor, and four gymnasts, myself included. I roomed with Anca, and Christina Itu and Angela Bratu were next door to us. The others were located across the landing. The accommodation was comfortable and private and we never felt isolated from other people, as we do on some of our overseas visits. Whether watching a Glenda Jackson and Walter Matthau movie in the local cinema, or going for a swim in the hot spa waters, we were able to mix freely with other residents and locals. The same was true in the evenings; we could sneak out to the local disco and enjoy a relaxed atmosphere. Many top Romanian sports personalities were staying at the Belvedere at the time, including another Olympic gold medallist, Corneliu Ion, the pistol shooter, with whom I struck up a holiday friendship. About the only time when things got serious was when we underwent neuro-muscular treatment and physiotherapy, a daily session lasting about an hour and a half.

We had a large table near the entrance to the restaurant, and were seldom bothered by others; I ate three cooked meals every day and yet my weight when I returned to Bucharest was the same as that on the day I left for Felix: 47 kilos. Most of my teammates had to endure a more restricted diet. For breakfast, I'd often gorge on fried eggs on hot cascaval cheese preceded by soured milk, followed by tea and occasionally supplemented by a ham and cheese roll! Anca would often have the same, but the others were not allowed cooked food. Their weight was still volatile, as mine had been in 1978, and their food intake had to be carefully controlled.

For dinner, one of my favorite dishes was veal *cordon bleu,* which, once again, hardly conforms to the conventional woman gymnast's diet. The "rule" is for a high protein diet with plenty of fresh vegetables, and just enough carbohydrates to convert into energy and then to be burned off. There is little chance of developing surplus fat that way, and in the mid to late teens, weight is of critical importance to a woman gymnast's ability to perform without undue stress on her body. It was a rule that I broke with impunity.

Having Graham Buxton Smither as a guest meant that I was free to indulge another of my passions, strictly forbidden to my teammates. A condition of his visits is that he brings with him a large supply of Mars bars and white chocolate! When our coach is not around, I do sometimes slip a few in the direction of my teammates. I hope he never reads this!

Add the odd chocolate bar, then some sweet, black coffee, and a few bottles of Pepsi and you have a fair picture of my normal diet. I would hardly win medals for boozing, but I enjoy the occasional glass of wine, champagne, or Martini. I don't go for strong alcoholic drinks, not even *palinka,* a lethal homemade variation on plum-brandy, so favored by many of our older friends. It's superb for stripping varnish from wood, I'm told!

8

TRAVELING WITH our national teams all over the world has not
only been an honor, but has led to many humorous, and sometimes
serious, incidents. There have been so many overseas trips that it is
difficult to remember all of them. However, I recall that my very first
one was in July 1971 to Ljubljana, Yugoslavia. This was a club competition and among the members of our team were my friends Georgeta
Gabor and Mariana Constantin. It ended in victory for us, and I found
myself in first place with a score of 38·50. It was a most successful debut.

It was on this trip that I started doll collecting, for when Marta and I
passed a tourist shop, I caught sight of a doll in Slovenian national
costume. I bought it with some pocket money that I'd managed to save.
I carried it in my arms all the way back to Romania on the train. It
meant at least as much as the medals. When I got back home, it took
pride of place in my room. The trouble was that it looked lonely, so I
decided that when I next went abroad I would get some company for it.
Although I have now stopped buying them for myself, people still give
me dolls. The largest that I have ever received is an eight foot, pink and
white teddy bear. Not surprisingly, it dominates the front room of our
home.

1972 was the year of the Olympic Games, though we saw little of
what went on as we were holidaying on the Black Sea coast during that
period. It was a year in which we went to Bulgaria and Hungary to
compete in full internationals, and in both events I found myself
returning to Onesti with a fair complement of gold medals and new
dolls.

At this time we were traveling within Eastern Europe, and 1973 saw
us competing in Warsaw. I remember that well, for it was a hot sunny
month of May, and I fell in love with a strange looking pair or shoes.
They were a form of traditional peasant footwear, gaily patterned with

83

those toe pieces that curl upwards. Though I could not wear them, I loved looking at them.

My first visit to Western Europe was in 1973 – to Mestre in Italy. It is a town close to Venice, and Bela allowed us a brief tour of that historic city. I can remember thinking that the one job I would never like would be a street cleaner in Venice – far too wet! It was that visit that Teodora was barred from, as I described earlier.

Of our tours in 1974, it is the Paris gymnastics demonstration that sticks most firmly in my mind, as it was the most chaotic and unpredictable I ever experienced. It had been an exciting year, starting with a visit from teams from Denver, Colorado and Poland to compete in Onesti. Then we went on to Korea, for the Phenian Friendship Tour, though an injury prevented me from participating fully in the competition. That didn't matter too much because the team won and Teodora did very well indeed. So, we eventually arrived in Paris in October.

We'd had very little warning of the event; the French Federation telephoned Nicu as head of our Federation saying they were in desperate need of a couple of extra bodies to make up the numbers. It was evidently an important occasion, because the top Soviet gymnast, Ludmilla Tourishcheva, was going to be present. The decision by our Federation to send Bela with Teodora and myself was a surprise, as Alina Goreac, the National Champion, was the obvious choice. When Bela came across to our apartment to give my parents and I the news he was in a very excitable mood. He could not keep still for a moment. Once she had heard, neither could my mother. We had to take the train to Bucharest the following day, pick up our passports and visas, and leave for Paris one day later. Within minutes of Bela's arrival, there was a knock at the front door, and Teodora rushed in, to see if I'd received the same invitation. For the next couple of hours we chatted excitedly as we packed our cases. Neither of us slept much that night. In fact, everything was a blur until we boarded the jet that was to take us to Le Bourget . . . I slept through most of the short journey. It was just as well, for the others told me later that it had been very rough.

When we arrived, there was another surprise in store for us – there was no one to meet us. Bela marched off to the airport information desk which put out a call, but still nobody showed. Bela was getting more and more impatient and angry. He opened up one of our bags and took out a training-suit top with "Romania" across its back in the hope that somebody would come to our aid. It was already early evening, and the competitions were due to start soon.

At last, some guy came ambling towards us. He had been sent by the organizers, and mercifully spoke Romanian. To Teodora and me it all seemed an exciting adventure, but Bela was less than delighted. We were bundled into a waiting car, and sped through a maze of traffic. After what seemed an endless succession of red lights, near collisions with taxis, and wild oaths from our driver, we pulled up outside the main hall.

'Right you two, wait in the car till we get back,' yelled Bela rushing into the hall with our interpreter. We sat in the back making faces into the driving mirror, and staring at the sort of clothes that the passers-by were wearing. I can remember being shocked at the number of young men with very long hair. It was not a familiar sight in Romania. About five minutes later, Bela re-emerged brandishing a foul temper, and shouting angrily at our luckless interpreter.

Bela explained to us that the organizers had not expected two such young gymnasts; they had expected a senior national like Alina. They therefore had decided to send us to a secondary competition in another hall, some distance away. The same thing had obviously happened to the Bulgarians as we followed their team to the little school gymnasium where we were to work out. By this time it was nearing six o'clock and the main event would be starting in a few hours. Bela decided there and then that once we'd taken part in the minor competition he would try and fiddle us into the main competition.

The hall was sparsely equipped, the auditorium even more sparsely populated. The atmosphere reeked of cigarette smoke; ever since, I have really disliked the stench of French cigarettes. Anyway, we did our routines in the hall, extracting some very genuine applause from the tiny but appreciative audience.

But Bela was not going to let us rest on our laurels. As soon as the results were announced, he literally collared our guide, propeled him towards the car and instructed him to drive us to the main competition hall.

That meant another crazy, zig-zagging ride across the center of Paris. Somehow we made it in one piece and arrived only five minutes after the event was due to begin.

The next hurdle was getting through the entrance to the building. The staff on the door were not prepared to let us in, because we had no tickets. They must have thought that we were just some kids trying to sneak in with their father as I'm sure we didn't look like their idea of international gymnasts. Our poor interpreter had gone ahead of us into the hall to speak with the organizers of the competition. However, Bela had no intention of waiting for the outcome of our interpreter's efforts. Remembering his days as a rugby player, he told us to stick close to him and charged his way past the crowds into the competition arena. We were in, but what now!

The vault was already in progress, and all three of us hid behind a large pile of crash-mats. Bela disppeared into the direction of the competition controller, and told us to stay put. But Bela was unable to change the attitudes of the organizers; they simply refused to allow us to join in the competition. He was livid. He had come all this distance to see us compete against the best gymnasts in a major Western event, and now he was being told to go away. He rejoined us behind the mats. We were all still wearing our leotards and track-suits under our coats, for there had been no time to change.

We heard the loudspeakers announce that the final vault was about to be executed by the undoubted star of the show, Tourischeva. Bela suddenly had an idea. As soon as Bela heard the roar of the crowd that signified the completion of Tourisheva's vault, he hissed, 'Right, Nadia, forget everything else, go and throw your Tsukahara. There's no time to measure out your run, but you ought to be able to gauge it by now. Stun them.'

I tore off my coat and track-suit, launched myself down the run and performed my Tsukahara. The officials were nonplussed, the audience erupted with loud applause, and I ran and hid behind the mats again. It was the first time that a Western competition had witnessed my vault version in a women's event. Perhaps understandably, Tourischeva was upset at the breach of order, because she, as the best-known gymnast present, expected to perform last on each piece of apparatus. She protested to the jury and threatened to leave the event if the program was not adhered to.

Hiding away from the searching eyes of the controllers, Teodora could not believe what was happening. I had complete faith in Bela's judgment, but I knew we were skating on thin ice. The auditorium was in uproar, and the organizers asked our interpreter to explain to the curious but enthusiastic onlookers who we were and where we were from. When he announced that I was only thirteen, the audience went wild.

The beam exercise was scheduled to follow. Bela was under strict orders to keep out of the arena, and more importantly, to keep me away from the apparatus. Tourischeva moved onto the beam and performed an elegant routine to great applause. Bela was watching her exercise by the side of the podium, and as soon as she had dismounted, he turned in our direction and beckoned me to mount the beam. I went through my well-rehearsed exercise to the bewilderment of the arena stewards, and to the delight of the crowd.

With the retirement of the great Soviet champion from the floor, the organizers relented. The whole atmosphere had changed and the audience wanted to see more of us, to know more about us. Bela was suddenly given permission for Teodora and me to put on an improvised joint floor display. Due to the mad rush, our music had been left in our cases which were still outside the main hall. The music was fetched and our program went down very well with everyone, including the organizers. Bela was delighted; he knew that he had been right to throw us in the deep end.

On his way back to Romania there was no doubt in his mind that we stood a better chance than ever of winning medals at the European Championships the following year.

We didn't get a chance to see much of Paris on that visit, Bela kept us on a short rein. That wasn't unusual in the early days and the close supervision continued until well after Montreal. Mind you, despite the lack of freedom, there were still some unusual moments to liven the routine of competition and exhibition.

One of the more ridiculous incidents happened in West Germany in 1977. Bela, Marta, Teodora, Marilena Neacsu, myself and a couple of others had gone there to put on four demonstrations in various towns. On one of the visits, I can't now remember which town, we arrived at the exhibition hall to find no one there who knew anything about our program. We were due to perform on the following day, so we were curious to know where our accommodation was. We were all looking forward to a good night's sleep. The hall was deserted but for a few cleaners, and freezing cold. The cleaners must have been waxing the floor rather too well, for they kept slipping. It was difficult to keep a straight face as these ladies kept hitting the deck.

That night we had to sleep in the changing room – hardly dream accommodation. Bela valiantly tried every trick in the book to get us some decent rooms for that night. In view of the low temperature in the hall and the changing room, Bela maintained that I was suffering from a fever. He complained to the hall manager that the organization was a joke, and that his top competitor was ill with a bad fever that would be made worse if we were forced to sleep in the changing room.

His scheme did not have quite the desired effect. The manager immediately hit the telephone and called not a hotel, or the Gymnastics Federation, but a local doctor who was asked to come and attend me. When the doctor finally arrived, Bela and I decided it would not be in the best interests of German-Romanian relations to let him examine me.

As a result, the tall, dark-suited doctor spent a merry hour chasing me around the gym hall, brandishing a thermometer. After about the third circuit, he decided it simply wasn't worth the effort. 'If she can run like that then there can't be that much wrong with her and if I can't examine her, what the hell can I do?' were his parting words.

It proved a dreadfully cold and uncomfortable night, despite the fact that we were all wrapped in as many layers of clothing and blankets as could be mustered. I was awakened in the morning by a tremendous crash and a high-pitched scream. Bela, in trying to leave the changing-room discreetly, had slipped on that highly polished floor and had fallen onto Teodora, breaking one of her fingers in the process. After that little incident, we all agreed there wasn't much else that could go wrong. For once, we were right.

Another incident I now look back on with a smile, although at the time it didn't seem very funny, happened in February '76 during a kind of pre-Olympic American tour calling at Toronto, Tucson, Albuquerque, San Francisco, and Denver. From the point of view of gymnastics, Toronto was a high spot for me. In the competition there, I achieved a record score of 79·75 out of a possible 80. Although the perfect scores I received in Toronto were not my first, I think I was overmarked in several instances.

The incident occurred while we were in San Francisco. It was our first night in the hotel and after a full day's traveling, we all retired to our rooms early. Teodora and I were sharing. We had gotten into our pajamas and had been watching a spot of TV, but none of the shows seemed particularly interesting, so we switched off and turned in for the night.

One of the most pleasant things about living in rural areas of Romania is that nobody worries about the possibility of theft or burglary. We were used to leaving the keys on the outside of our doors in hotels, even while we were asleep, as this allowed Bela to keep a watchful eye on us easily. That night, he asked us to leave the key in the door as usual, and without thinking we did so.

Round about midnight, the door opened slowly and a shaft of light awoke me from my sleep. I could just about make out the shape of a person entering the room very stealthily. I don't know why, but I was not nervous, just curious to see who it was.

The entrance to the bathroom was next to my bed and I slid out, turning on the light. Moving towards the centre of the room was a tall, long-haired man. He was wearing jeans and a black leather jacket. He was also wearing sneakers, which is why we hadn't heard him entering the room. He had our keys in his right hand, and wore gloves on both hands. He stopped between the two beds and looked startled to find himself in the company of two diminutive girls.

'Who are you? what are you doing here?' I shouted in English. He said nothing, just looked quite baffled. At that moment Teodora woke up and started screaming the same question in Romanian. He began to back off towards the door.

Our intruder seemed as keen to see the back of us as we were of him. Just as he backed out into the corridor, I grabbed the keys from his hand, dived back into the room and locked the door behind me. Teodora was hiding under the sheets and a muffled voice asked if everything was safe. I jumped into my bed, leaving the bathroom light on and began to tremble.

For all we knew, we could have been murdered in our sleep that night. Needless to say, neither of us slept a wink after that. We eventually drifted into a sort of exhausted trance, but both jumped violently when there was a loud bang on the door the following morning. It was Bela, of course, checking that we were up for breakfast and surprised to find he could not open the door.

I called out, 'Who's there, what do you want?' in English. Bela's impatient voice was clearly audible, and we both ran to unlock the door.

'You two look terrible. Why the hell didn't you get any sleep? I thought I could trust you to go to bed without having to check up on you.'

When we explained what had happened the previous night and gave him a gory description of our mysterious intruder, he looked most alarmed.

'I'm sorry girls. It's my fault really. This is not Onesti, it's a big American city. You'd better lock your door in future!'

At least we got an extra lie-in that day thanks to our midnight caller. We never did discover exactly what he was up to.

Many things have happened to us on our travels, and one of my favourite experiences occurred in Bologna. Our team from the 23rd August Park had traveled there in the company of Mili and Nicu as well as all the coaches. Mili had decided we should enjoy a little relaxation. We sat in her room and tried to decide what best to do. Eventually it was agreed that we'd go to the movies, so Mili, who speaks fluent Italian, picked up a local newspaper and checked to see what was showing. Because so many of the girls in our squad were very young, it had to be something that would be suitable for all of us. Mili knew how much we loved rock music and dancing, so when she mentioned *Saturday Night Fever* we were all happy to agree.

We arrived late for the performance, but we did not mind. The second half of *Fever* had just started, and we settled in our seats, many of us with an ice-cream, to watch what we had told Mili was a film all about disco-dancing. However, some of the love scenes near the end of the film were quite passionate. Mili became very uncomfortable because she was worried that the youngest members of the squad might be upset by them. What she considered "adult entertainment" was not something any of us were terribly bothered about and most of the girls were giggling at the scenes. I suppose that's what the so-called "generation gap" is all about. Anyway, we all enjoyed the movie and the music.

1978 was a difficult year for me as a certain amount of upheaval in my personal life threatened to overshadow my gymnastics.

At the age of sixteen and a half I had become aware that there was more to life than gymnastics – I had also reached a stage when I started to question the way of life I had always taken for granted before. It was a period when my weight was causing me enormous problems; everything seemed to be happening at once. On top of all this, I was far removed from the security of my family, because I was now living in Bucharest. The critics wrote me off as a competitor, but I knew them to be wrong.

9

IT ALWAYS seems to annoy journalists and interviewers that I don't have any particularly edifying remarks to make about my rivals, colleagues and predecessors in international gymnastics.

Quite simply, I don't think about other competitors much, let alone worry about them. This is not an attitude inspired by arrogance or self-esteem but the fact that gymnastics is still one of the most unpredictable sports there is. I would hate to have to bet on the outcome of any major competition, because (thank Goodness!) with determination, the will to win and supreme belief in his or her own abilities, any one of a number of leading gymnasts is capable of taking the honors on the day. That's why it is still all down to worrying about your own form and performance, and all the careful assessment of the opposition in the world can't substitute for self-confidence and tip-top physical condition. About the only time I give my rivals much thought is when I'm lying below top position mid-way through a competition, and I need to try to spot any weaknesses in the gymnasts ahead of me that might be worth exploiting.

Most leading gymnasts would be considered outrageously inconsistent by the standards of many other sports. That is the nature of the beast. Take Shaposhnikova or Filatova, for example; they are both superb gymnasts (they would not have gotten into as strong a team as the Russians if they were anything less than superb), but they are prone to error under the kind of pressure that is nowadays part and parcel of a major tournament.

Undoubtedly the best-known gymnast who was prone to wilt under the strain of tough competiton was Olga Korbut. As a person, she seemed pleasant and highly individual, though I always think of her as a rather stronger actress, playing to her audience, than competitor. Her personality radiated where her technical ability sometimes let her down, though if her lasting achievement is that she made gymnastics more entertaining, more enjoyable for many more people, that is something she's entitled to feel very proud about.

Consistency is the key to regular success in competition, which explains the lack of opposition Olga gave me during our first "confrontation" at the Montreal Olympics. Gymnastics fans had been waiting for our encounter with eager anticipation, but the titanic struggle that some had hoped for never really materialized.

I associate Tourischeva with the "old school" of gymnastics, exhibiting a minimum of risk but a maximum of elegance, grace, artistry, poise and phenomenal sportsmanship, all of which she displayed magnificently at Montreal. Now she is a very fine coach.

The one rival that caused me more sleepless nights than any other was my teammate, Teodora. One year my senior, and in the days prior to Montreal my best friend, she was my closest rival and had beaten me several times before. Her performance at the Canadian Olympics proved that she was a very worthy competitor, and that I had been right to watch her very, very carefully.

I suppose when people think back over the classic gymnastics rivalries of the last four or five years, they remember my many great tussles with Nelli Kim. She is, without doubt, a very fine and artistic gymnast, and her winning vault at Montreal was out of this world. We have a healthy respect for each others' abilities (at least, I have a healthy respect for hers!), though Nelli is now nearing the end of her competitive career.

The emphasis on technical superiority which is the modern trend has given rise to a new generation of gymnasts that display great virtuosity, but perhaps not enough soul. I am aware that that is something I was continually being accused of when I was younger, and if I am partly to blame I regret it. Maxi Gnauck is a good example of this new breed; she is best known for her bars work, which is clinically precise and immaculate, but whether it contains the strong artistic appeal or the excitement of some of our predecessors I don't know. She is continuing in the Jahn mold of technical rather then interpretive virtuosity which, I suppose, is a Germanic trait.

But for her tragic accident, Elena Mukhina would surely have continued as one of my toughest opponents; in many ways our styles and approaches to the sport were very similar.

People usually forget that gymnastics is one of the most international of the internationally popular spectator sports. Unlike, say, tennis or boxing, the sport is not at all dominated by athletes from countries with a similar culture and a common language, and despite the fact that there is a very active gymnastic "circuit", we don't really find it possible to get to know each other on a personal level. Language, plus the inevitable isolation that comes from the need to be protective of young competitors, creates barriers, particularly at major events. Our brief exchanges of friendship and respect are, sadly, difficult to maintain.

10

ONE OF the things that I found most difficult to adjust to after moving to Bucharest in 1978 was the lack of countryside. I'd gotten used to spending time away from my family by now, but it still made me sad not to have them near me. Father would sometimes drive down from Onesti to see me at weekends, but even this was a rarity. I was moved in order to allow me more freedom and because I'd become rebellious under Bela and Marta's tight supervision.

It would be wrong to suggest that I was a poor defenseless little creature having to be protected from a sadistic, overbearing coach. It was not like that at all. Anyone who understood the personalities of Bela and myself could have predicted the problems that would eventually occur. Like the parents of many teenagers, Bela could not accept that I was now grown up and needed at least a semblance of control over my own life. Despite the later disagreements with him, Bela played an essential part in my success and whatever our recent differences, I owe him very much. One lasting quality he gave me, as I mentioned earlier, was self-discipline. However, that did not stop us from arguing about almost everything. In the gymnastics hall, most of our conflict centered around the style of my exercises, and the sort of training they required.

'This is ridiculous, I'm not making those stupid little gestures in my floor exercise – they might look very cute on a child of ten, but they look foolish and phoney on me. Do I look like a child?' I asked Bela, infuriated by his desire for gamine characteristics in my work.

'Well, you're certainly behaving like one, moaning all the time. You don't know what's best for you, and we do. Stop arguing and do as you are told, for once. I don't have time for prima donnas in my group. Get on with it!' shouted Bela in reply.

'What's the point if all that does is make me look silly? It's the judges

95

that we have to impress, not little old ladies in the audience. I'm damned if I am going to make a spectacle of myself.'

By now, we were both losing our tempers. 'What do you think you are doing now if you are not making a spectacle of yourself. Get out until you have cooled down and are ready to apologize. I am not going to allow you to disrupt the smooth running of this hall!'

This argument was typical of the many that we had, and Bela was right – I should not have disrupted the classes. But neither of us could help ourselves, because we both felt that the other was wrong. My family was informed of these difficulties and my mother was upset by what she saw as a lack of loyalty and gratitude on my part for all that Bela had done for me. I think my father appreciated that I had reached the age when I would have to be given room to spread my wings a bit. Sadly, on top of other pressures, a serious domestic one had begun to develop, for my mother and father were starting to argue a lot with each other. Though I did not know it at the time, things were going to get worse between them.

Since I'd become a world class gymnast a lot of changes had been made in our lifestyle. My father had remained largely unaffected by this, but my mother had found it more difficult to accept. Unlike father, who was quite content with his way of life, my mother's expectations had been raised and it was obvious she would no longer be satisfied for herself or Adrian with things as they stood. My parents just grew further and further apart. As father became more depressed by the increasing schism between mother and himself, he found solace in drinking more heavily, I suppose to deaden the pain. In the end divorce became inevitable. When it came through I felt very relieved. This might at first seem like an odd reaction to the splitting up of one's parents, both of whom I love dearly, but there came a point where it really seemed the best thing for both of them. The moment my father was on his own he stopped drinking and nowadays he is a much happier man. The relationship between mother and me is much happier now that we are together in our new home in Bucharest. Things do have a habit of working themselves out.

It was during my first stay at the 23rd August Sports Complex that my life went through a series of profound changes. These were both personal and concerned with my sport. Even though we lived most of our life within the confines of the sports complex, the very fact that it was in the capital meant that an incredible range of activities and interests was open to me for the first time in my life. Perhaps at this point I should describe a typical day in my gymnastics life.

The sports hostel is about 50 meters from the training hall. It has

three floors, with the restaurant on the ground floor, just inside the front entrance. Teodora and I shared a room on the second floor at the far end of the corridor. Coincidentally, they put me in the same room again when I returned to Bucharest in 1980. Generally, we would get up at about seven o'clock in the morning, and pop into the restaurant for a light breakfast. It had to be very light, for we started training at half past eight. Normally, I would have a cup of tea with lemon, and a cheese roll. I often stashed another roll in my training bag, which I would munch surreptitiously when my coaches weren't around.

The first half hour of the session would be devoted entirely to warming up. Suppling and stretching exercises must be carried out in advance of serious training, because, if the body is stiff and cold, it is very easy to injure yourself.

At the beginning of a warm up, we tend to look like something out of *Close Encounters,* being covered in several layers of track suits zipped right up to the chin and barely recognizable as a result. As we get warmed, we gradually peel off down to our leotards, footless tights, socks, gym slippers, and probably a T-shirt.

Generally, a warm-up starts with a run around the perimeter of the floor area, sometimes with a high knee action, sometimes swivelling from the hips keeping the legs straight. While we run, we will either circle our arms or swing them and rotate our torsos. After two or three minutes this loosens you up. Once warm and with our muscles loosened we will try stretching exercises, getting down on haunches, straightening and stretching one leg, then switching to the other. Lying back and supporting ourselves on our elbows, we start rotating each leg from the hip then do our own thing for a few minutes to sort out any individual aches and pains. The last thing I always do before working out on the first piece of apparatus is to lean with my back across the beam and, stretching my arms behind my head, lean back, until my feet almost leave the ground. That really loosens up my back.

After the warm up, a typical training session would start with our coaches announcing the order in which we will practise on the apparatus. At the 23rd August Park Gymnastics Hall, we're lucky enough to have a good ratio of pupils to coaching staff. There are five gymnasts under the direction of two coaches and a choreographer. Our national men's squad trains in the same hall and often at the same time as us, and occasionally we get to borrow one of their coaches. Training at the same time as the men causes no particular problems except maybe when we are warming up, or working, on the floor area and they are also trying to warm up. Staying on the floor when the men are warming up is like dicing with death for the girls, because the men prepare by playing soccer with a fury, as though the fate of the world hung on the outcome. If you've ever been hit by a super-charged tennis ball you may be able to imagine what it feels like to stop one with your thigh, or stomach, or face!

What makes the whole situation more precarious is that the balance beams are placed along two of the sides of this large green carpeted battle zone – a ball whizzing past your nose does tend to play havoc with your poise on the apparatus. If we are due to work on our vaulting, we will all use the apparatus together, but generally we split into two groups. For instance, three of us might be working on the beams while the other two would be battling with the asymmetric bars. We are all given a set number of exercises or elements and combinations to perform before changing around. Having completed a work out on all the apparatus, we might find ourselves being asked to execute the dance elements of our floor work, with the acrobatic parts to follow in the next training session. It is here that the choreographer comes into his or her own. If, after all of this, there is still some time and energy left, we may use it on some ballet disciplines or perhaps some general toning and conditioning exercises. At the end of a session, after checking with our coaches, we are free to leave.

Another important thing that we do in these training periods is sit down and work out with our coaches the new elements and exercises that need to be incorporated in our routines and perfected in time for the next big international events. This is no simple task. Sometimes a gymnast is the innovator of a new move, though it tends to be inspired by the coach. The gymnast then has to be convinced that she can do it, and that can take a lot of persuasion at times. It does depend a lot on the sort of working relationship that exists between coach and pupil. Out will come a copy of the "Code of Points" which will be consulted carefully, especially when the idea is to put together a series of elements in order to create a new combination. Each must have its difficulty tariff checked to see how many points the combination is worth and to insure that the new routine gives the gymnast the opportunity to shoot for the highest possible marks.

The ratings are graded as 'A' for easy, 'B' for a medium difficulty, and 'C' for superior difficulty, on top of which may be added certain bonus points. Generally, if you combine two elements of the same value directly to each other, their value is raised to the next tariff. When these are both 'C' elements, they become 'Cr', which denotes the addition of risk and carries the maximum possible value. Some elements of exceptional difficulty carry the 'Cr' value on their own. An 'A' is worth 0·20 points, 'B' is 0·40, and 'C' is 0·60.

The optional, or voluntary, exercises are marked out of a maximum 10·00 points. This is composed of a possible 3·00 for the difficulties, a 0·50 bonus for originality and risk, 2·50 for the combination of the elements into an exercise, and 4·00 for execution and virtuosity. It is the scoring of the last section that gives rise to most of the disputes for this is the area of greatest risk of subjective judging in the entire sport.

The introduction of a completely new element allows a gymnast the vanity of having it named after him or her. On the asymmetric bars, the world has me to thank or blame for the Comaneci Somersault and the Comaneci Dismount. The somersault is my version of the Radochla, and is performed entirely on the high bar. It is a forwards somersault, in the straddle position, from the high bar to re-grasp on the high bar, which means that the gymnast doesn't get to see the bar while trying to catch it until the last possible moment. My dismount involved an underswing on the high bar, with a half turn before executing a tucked backward somersault to land. Nowadays, I execute a full turn in the *salto* to gain a risk value. Both of these elements were worked out between Bela and myself, each being confident in the ability of the other.

These days, ideas for new moves in my exercises tend to come from me; when I have thought them through, I then seek the reaction of Anca and Gheorghe Gorgoi. They will concentrate on assessing its technical feasibility and suitability, and the choreographer might add her comments as to its artistic merit. I am very fortunate in that I am able to visualize the mechanics of a movement in my mind's eye.

At times, the repetitiveness of training make concentration and enjoyment difficult to maintain, but you need to keep at it. A gymnast who does not train seriously does herself a disservice. She does not deserve the attention of a coach. It is all a question of attitude, and self-discipline. We're generally allowed to have pop music playing in the background to break up the monotony of our sessions. It does seem to make a big difference, even though some of the coaches may not share our musical tastes. All the gymnasts are young people, and the music reflects our youth and creates a relaxed, harmonious atmosphere.

The arbitrary choice of background music for training sessions is far removed from the meticulous task of putting together music for a floor exercise. First, I and my choreographer agree the overall style of the exercise, and then we carefully select various pieces of music that fit the bill. The gymnast's opinion always is most important in this, because it is she, and no one else, that must perform to the chosen music. If it does not match her temperament and physique, it will adversely affect the exercise.

The right pieces of music having been selected, the sound studios take over, armed with a stop watch to make sure that the exercise runs within the permitted limits of 1.10 secs. and 1.30 secs. and on the mixing console the *allegri* are skillfully blended with the *andantes*. After that, it is down to laborious, painstaking practise on the floor, day after day. Refinements will be added in practise until the new routine is ready to be revealed to the judges at the next international.

A training session would last until about eleven o'clock, when we return to the hostel for a short break, before going to our first academic classes of the day. My favorite subject was English which, next to my own, is my favorite language. In Romania, most young people pick up a little bit of English from the rock music that we all listen to, and the British and American shows on Romanian TV. There are always sports teams and individuals leaving on a tour abroad and they make sure to return with heaps of foreign magazines and paperbacks.

Lunch, at about one o'clock, would be followed by more school lessons and a short break before returning to the training hall at four thirty. The evening session would last until eight, at which time we'd slink back, wearily, to the restaurant and then to our rooms.

After a long shower I used to make a hot, sweet, and very strong cup of coffee and then sit down to my homework. If there was something particularly interesting on TV, we'd visit the TV room and relax with a Pepsi for an hour or so. It was always a good place to meet friends and trade horror stories about the way that our respective coaches were making us suffer. Otherwise we might just stay in our rooms reading fashion magazines and listening to music. I used to spend a lot of my spare time either taping my favorite tracks from some of the boys' record albums, or digging up something I'd be prepared to swap, especially at competitions, for some Abba, Boney M, Bee Gees, or ELO cassettes.

Not many of the fashions we admired from foreign magazines find their way over to Romania. As gymnasts, we seem to spend most of our time in light, warm, and comfortable garments like track-suits, which seem to be quite fashionable at the moment. When I am away from the gym-hall, I tend to lounge in comfortable clothes like track-suit pants and tee-shirts.

We all love to wear jeans, for these are both stylish and functional and can be worn anywhere. I tend to look out for genuine American jeans as they seem to last the longest. I also really like soft and natural clothes and I own several pairs of satin trousers, and quite a few silk shirts. However, I don't get the chance to wear smarter clothes very often, except to official functions and parties.

Footwear is the thing that we have to be most wary of. Many of the fashion shoes that I see other girls or women wearing would not meet with the approval of our doctors. I spend most of my time in gym slippers or training shoes, but when I am dressing to go out, I enjoy putting on shoes which have a heel on them. The few times in my life that I have tried high-heels, I have to admit I found walking in them tougher than balancing on the beam!

One of the big differences between Onesti, and later Deva, and the center in Bucharest was that the men's team also trained in the same hall, an enormous room split into two sections. At the back of the hall is the men's area with all their apparatus except the vault run, floor area, and tumbling strip which are shared between us. The rest of it is given over to us. Although we preferred to keep out of their way when the men were limbering up, it was fun having them around the place. When I arrived there for the first time, I'd just reached an age when boys started to notice me. Being a year older, Teodora tended to be more outgoing when it came to making friends with the opposite sex. I was still pretty reserved in other people's company.

As I got used to my new surroundings, I began to relax more, and Teodora and I used to go along to parties, listen to the latest sounds and dance a little. None of the coaches knew about these parties, which was just as well as they'd have hit the roof at the thought. Sometimes our parties went on late into the night, and we had to use a lookout to check for prowling members of staff or coaches in the corridor. After the party, there was always the challenge of sneaking back up to our rooms without being heard or spotted.

It was during this period that my often commented upon friendship with Kurt Szilier, one of our top gymnasts, started. There have been a lot of unfounded stories on the subject; the simple truth was that for some time Kurt was my boyfriend and we loved being in each other's company. It was all part of growing up – something the gossipmongers seemed incapable of understanding. Contrary to popular belief, my body did not develop overnight. It happened gradually – over the two years between Montreal and Strasbourg – but because I was not seen that often internationally, and everyone remembered me from 1976, the natural change in my physique came as quite a shock. They simply had not witnessed the continuous process.

All those stories about my being administered vast amounts of ovulatory suppressants to retard puberty were ridiculous. The story ran that after Montreal, the drugs no longer needed to be given to me (presumably because I had completed my "allotted" task!), and with their withdrawal I crashed into unsuspecting womanhood. Undeniably, I reached puberty rather later than is normal, but this is a common result of the somewhat unusual relationship between the diet and work output of a competitive athlete. It is a natural reaction within the body, related to total fat content and the hormonal change that it induces, and not drug-created.

In gymnastics, the power-to-weight ratio of a competitor, whether a man or woman, is of great importance. Long levers and suppleness have their part to play, but keeping weight down to a safe workable minimum is a particular necessity for women. At the age of most top female gymnasts, which is in the mid to late teens, natural changes in the body can make it difficult to keep weight in check at times. By balancing the calorie input, represented by food, and the calorie output, represented by physical and emotional effort, an increase in weight can be prevented.

When this dietary approach is applied to a girl before she passes puberty, it will tend to delay its onset slightly. The natural mechanisms of the body cause the hormonal changes that will produce this effect, without need of drugs or artificial aids. The simple fact is that it is difficult for an overweight gymnast to work; no matter how competent a performer she is, she can never move with grace and elegance. My own problems in '78, when I was overweight, sorted themselves out quite normally in the course of time.

One of the first things I noticed about my new-found maturity was additional self-confidence as well as a self-consciousness about my appearance. The time had come to pay more attention to eye makeup and nail polish, to be more thoughtful about hairstyles. When it came to my hair, I tended to fall back on what was functional for gymnastics rather than what was particularly stylish. It is only recently that fashion has had anything to do with my appearance. My recent decision to have my hair permed seems to have met with the approval of my friends and family – I must admit, I like it.

At first nobody recognized the new "made up" Nadia; I remember Graham, (my English friend), walking straight past me in the training hall. It took a while before I realized that make up is supposed to enhance good features, not dominate them. Nowadays I find that my tastes are getting a bit more conservative and sophisticated than they were a few years back. One thing that Anca has is very good dress sense, and she and I can spend ages talking about clothes, if not actually looking at them through shop windows. Anca is often affectionately called "her ladyship" because of the elegant way she moves and dresses. I couldn't wish for a better teacher.

I really love dancing and enjoy the open-air discos that we go to when we're by the Black Sea in summertime. One of the first things we investigate on arriving at a new venue on foreign tours is the whereabouts of the nearest disco. Our coaches don't object to discos, in fact they can often be persuaded to join us, especially after a few drinks! Modern dancing really is a perfect way of keeping fit.

I'm also crazy about the movies, especially American and British films, which we sometimes get to see at special showings at some of our sports centers. When I was younger my heart-throb was Alain Delon, but tastes change, and at the moment my favorite film star is Robert Redford, though I have to share him with most of the other girls! It is a pity that we seldom get visits by international entertainment figures in Romania, though I still remember the visit to Onesti some years ago of an American TV crew with a 'lunatic' called Flip Wilson, who got up to all sorts of antics in the gym hall.

Having a coach that recognizes and tolerates my independent streak has placed me in a fortunate position in comparison to some of the gymnasts that I know.

If I had to point to a single event that could be said to have changed my life it would have to be the 1976 Montreal Olympic Games. As far as my performance was concerned, there was nothing particularly unusual about that tournament, but unquestionably it represented the moment when I suddenly had to begin sharing my gymnastics, which had always been a fairly private experience previously, with the rest of the world.

What the team and I managed to accomplish at Montreal was the result of years of careful preparation, but the audience in the Hall, and throughout the TV world had not noticed us before and reacted pretty wildly to what it saw. It seemed impossible to convince the world's press that our success was the result of patient work rather than a momentary flash of inspiration. To some extent, the repetition and monotony of training for such a major event had taken the edge off of my enthusiasm for the Games. But my desire to prove myself on the apparatus was strong and I got tremendous satisfaction from performing to the best of my ability.

Despite all the arguments about nationalism in sports, it is impossible to forget at an event like the Olympic Games that you are competing for your country. This was not an aspect that Bela stressed to Teodora or myself in training or at Montreal. It was only at the flag raising ceremony with the Romanian National Anthem playing over the loudspeakers that we realized just how important our victory was to everybody back home.

11

THE JOURNEY to Montreal was uneventful though long. As usual Teodora slept through most of the flight. All the team members had been told to try and grab some sleep on the plane. We would need a few days to adjust to the time difference, Montreal time being eight hours behind us in Romania. We settled into our seats and I found myself thinking about home. I knew that my parents and other relatives would be staying up until the early hours of the morning to watch us compete for Olympic honors.

The team consisted of Bela and Marta, Anca, Georgeta, Gabriela Trusca, Mariana Constantin, Teodora and myself, with Marilena Neacsu and Luminita Mileas as reserves. Mili naturally accompanied us in the women's party, for she was one of the head Judges at the Games. Nicolae Vieru headed the men's party whose best gymnast, Dan Grecu, has recently retired to take up coaching following an injury in Moscow.

When we arrived at the Olympic Village, all we wanted to do was take a shower and relax. The Village consisted of four enormous apartment buildings, each nineteen stories high. In the sunshine they looked like two bright pyramids; I rather liked their design. What seemed difficult to believe was that they housed over 10,000 competitors and team officials. Three of the buildings were occupied by the men, the remaining one was for the much smaller number of women. Our apartment had three main rooms, and one bathroom. Having just one bathroom among all of us didn't work out very well as it caused no end of delays. As you entered the door, the room on the right was for Lia Manoliu, who was the Chief of the Romanian Team. Anca, Gabriella, and Marilena had the room on the left. That left Marta, myself, Teodora, Georgeta, and Mariana in the main room.

It was all pretty cramped and, as if that wasn't bad enough, Marta and Bela's constant supervision meant that the whole atmosphere became very claustrophobic.

Another thing I found difficult to get used to were the intense security arrangements. We all had to wear a special pass with our photograph on it. I wouldn't have recognized myself from my picture, but then my passport photograph doesn't look very much like me either. I'm not usually at my best first thing in the morning, and it always seems to work out that these pictures are taken then.

I had to present the pass whenever I wanted to enter, or leave, the apartment building. Whenever we left the Village we had to repeat the process at two separate points, and had to go through it yet again upon our return. In addition, at every entrance and exit, all our hand luggage was checked by electronic detectors. They must have been very sensitive, because the first time I tried to pass through they started beeping madly. Suddenly everybody's head turned in my direction and the guards began rifling through my belongings, presumably looking for a bomb or a machine gun. However, it was nothing more exciting than a large number of hand-guards – the buckles and studs must have set the machine off. I didn't make that mistake a second time.

There were lots of recreational facilities on offer to all participating at Montreal, but Bela had decided that we should not get distracted from the task at hand, and so we hardly had any opportunity to sample them. The International Center housed most of them, and it was one of the few places where outsiders, armed with a letter of validation from the appropriate team officials, could meet with competitors. There were boutiques, restaurants, a cinema, a library, and some swimming pools and tennis courts. Within the complex there were large communal rooms on each floor with televisions, music systems, and a selection of magazines and newspapers. There was even live entertainment available at various times of the day on the sun terrace in the International Center.

Not only did Bela forbid us to wander around; he kept a careful watch over our eating habits. None of us were allowed into the big international 24 hour restaurant located in the basement of one of the men's buildings unless we were accompanied by Bela, Marta, or Carmen Dumitru, the team doctor. It was a great pity, for they served dishes from all over the world, and everything was free. For the sake of keeping in perfect shape for the competition we had to forego the pleasure.

Actually, eating was a problem for two of our teammates. In Onesti we were used to a strictly controled diet, and our stomachs were conditioned to a small intake of solids. But Anca and Gabriela, who were both several years my seniors, did not train under the Karolys' system, and therefore felt miserable on such a meager diet. They received an adequate nutrient intake, but that did not prevent them from waking up every morning at five o'clock with pangs of hunger.

We were all eager to get on with the competition, and for the first few days of our stay, used some local school gymnasia to practise. It helped to keep us fit, but it wasn't really a substitute for the chance to work on the competition apparatus. On Tuesday July 13 we were at last driven to the Montreal Forum, which was where the competition was to begin five days later, the day after the Opening Ceremony. The Forum was situated about ten kilometers from the Village along a busy street, to be exact, at 2313 St Catherine Street West. It was not a new building, having been used for many years to host ice-hockey matches.

With us on that day were the teams from Russia, East Germany and Hungary. Bela was studying the Soviet women very closely, obviously looking for the slightest weakness that we might be able to exploit. They had a pretty formidable line-up: Tourischeva, Korbut, Kim, Saadi, Grozdova, and Filatova. The average age of their team was certainly a lot higher than ours which meant that most of them were more experienced.

Bela told us that it did not matter. 'There is only one thing that counts when it comes to the medals at the competition – who is the best person on the day. Don't let anyone's reputation intimidate you. All it means is that they used to be good. They have now got to prove that they still are.'

It seemed very good advice. Anyway, why should I worry? I'd met most of the Soviet gymnasts before, and had often gotten the better of them. When I left for the Games, I reckoned that I had a fair chance of picking up a couple of Individual Apparatus medals, and naturally I hoped for the gold.

I reckoned that the bars were my best bet for a medal. So did Bela. I also felt hopeful about the balance beam, as I'd fallen from it at the pre-Olympics and felt confident that lightning wouldn't strike a second time.

Watching the Russians working out was valuable, for it proved to all of us that they were fallible. Both Olga and Nelli fell from the beam, and none of the Russians looked happy on the bars. In fact, it was the Hungarian, Marta Egervari, who threatened to be our greatest rival on that apparatus. Bela was determined that his team should put on a good display in practice. This was not for the benefit of the press and public in the auditorium, but to put psychological pressure on the other teams present. I strongly suspect that the seeds of my individual success were sown during those training sessions. For I had faith in Bela's assumption that watching a fourteen and a half year old gymnast going through her routine with an impressive display of technical virtuosity would cause the most seasoned competitors to feel their years.

And finally the big day of the first competition came around. As usual it started with the Team Compulsory Exercises, followed by the Voluntaries. With my number "73" firmly sewn on to the back of my leotard, I prepared for my first discipline, the beam. For most gymnasts this is not an ideal piece to start with, as it requires a tremendous amount of control. But as far as I was concerned, it made no difference what I began on, for I had performed the same movement so many times in the past that it had almost become routine.

I heard the roar from the spectators greeting Olga's score of 9·90 for her bar work, and waited for Teodora to finish her beam exercise, for she was the last but one to compete – I had the distinction of bringing up the rear.

When I mounted the podium prior to beginning my exercise, I saw that all the members of the Soviet team had finished and were staring in my direction. Marta whispered to me to put on a good show for them and, receiving the green light from the judges' panel, I opened my Olympic account. The routine passed without anything untoward happening and, having dismounted, I rejoined my fellow competitors.

The judges flashed my score of 9·90 and there followed huge cheers from the audience. I remembered that I'd been told to respond in a friendly and smiling manner to the crowd, so back to the podium I ran and waved to them, which produced another burst of applause. We were giving the Russians a run for their money not only in gymnastics, but also in showmanship.

The floor exercise was next, and then the vault. There was nothing sensational about my own performances and I received marks of 9·75 and 9·70 respectively. What pleased me intensely was that I was due to finish on my favorite piece of apparatus – the asymmetric bars. Furthermore, I was going to be the last competitor on it, which gave me the chance of leaving a good impression on the audience and the judges to hold me in good stead for the Voluntaries the following Monday.

It was by now late in the evening. Although the competition had commenced at eight thirty that morning, because of the huge number of gymnasts involved, and the fact that the top teams are the last to go, we did not start until five o'clock.

Teodora chalked the bars for me with a palmful of magnesium carbonate, jumped down, leaving the stage to me. The whole thing flowed like a dream. I was unaware of time or effort. Almost instinctively, my body slipped into its well rehearsed sequence of movements culminating in a good dismount. I knew it had been a good performance even before the reaction of the spectators invaded my concentration. I jumped down after presenting to the Head Judge and was hugged by all the members of my team.

Suddenly an almighty roar went up and Dorina screamed in joy. I turned to look at the scoreboard – it showed that I had been awarded only one point! It registered 1·00, which in those days was the computer's way of announcing a perfect score. It was the first one in Olympic history. Pandemonium broke out around me, even other competitors rushed to congratulate me. I waved frantically at the cheering crowd before Bela could marshal the team together ready for the march out. The only team which did not seem to be sharing in the excitement was the Soviets, but they must have been satisfied with their Team Compulsory position, as they were leading us with a total of 194·20 to 192·70.

On the day of the Voluntary Exercises, it was again well into the evening before we started our routines. The order was the same as for the previous night, so I was first onto the beam, while the Russians worked on the bars. This was a chance to demonstrate my particular style of gymnastics and I knew that I could not go wrong. Nothing was going to stop me from demonstrating what I thought a beam exercise was all about. Nothing did. If at all possible, the audience seemed even more vociferous than the night before. The score came up – I'd been awarded my second 10·00. Bela and Marta were ecstatic. They had really proved themselves before the whole world.

I managed to catch Ludmilla Tourischeva's floor work, which was the epitomy of grace, and received a mark of 9·95. Elegance is always a delight to watch. Soon we had come round again to the bars, and it was my turn. The adrenalin flowed, as did the routine and once again I was given a perfect score. It wasn't possible for Romania to take the team title, but we captured the silver. We were having our most successful Olympic gymnastics competition ever and it quickly dawned on Bela that we had a very good chance of picking up a gold medal or two in the two remaining competitions – the Individual Apparatus Finals and the Overall Individual Final.

The result of the Team Competition was:

1: USSR	390·35
2: Romania	387·15
3: DDR	385·10

After the medal ceremony was over, I had to brave what I came to consider the worst of my ordeals in Montreal – the press conference. After receiving perfect scores, I was continually being sought out by reporters.

We had a free day before the Overall Final on Wednesday, 21. Teodora and I managed to slip away from the others and demolish two quarts of ice-cream and a couple of Cokes between us on the sun terrace. It was wicked, but very enjoyable. Dorina wolfed most of the ice-cream – she seems to have an insatiable appetite for the stuff.

It was quite an experience to sit around the common room in our team quarters and read reports of our successes in the newspapers. It was the aftermath of the Olympics that I was tagged "Little Miss Perfect". They should have looked at some of my maths exam papers!

Before I realized it, we were back in the hall for the Overall Individual competition. Under a new ruling teams were restricted to entering their top three gymnasts. That meant that Teodora, Mariana, and I represented Romania. For the Soviet Union there was Olga, Nelli, and Ludmilla. Everything looked set for a terrific battle. The previous day, the team doctor and our physiotherapist gave us a thorough workout.

I opened on the asymmetric bars this time, and notched up another perfect score. The scoring on the bars was generally high, with Dorina, Nelli, Olga, Ludmilla, and Marta Egervari of Hungary all being given 9·90. On the floor, Nelli was awarded 9·95, as was Ludmilla for her vault. When Nelli came to her Tsukahara with full twist, she delighted the crowd by scoring a perfect ten. My beam exercise scored another ten for me although my vault let me down with a score of only 9·85. By the time that I came to my final apparatus, I knew that I was a hair's breadth away from becoming Overall Olympic Champion. When 9·90 came up, it was all over.

However, what I had achieved only began to sink in as I climbed the victory rostrum and, with the gold medal around my neck, watched the Romanian flag rise majestically to the sound of our National Anthem. At that moment my thoughts were miles away in Onesti, and I wondered what my parents were thinking about all of this. The moment that most touched me during the medal ceremony was when Ludmilla, the woman I admired so much, came across to me before receiving her medal, shook my hand and kissed me on the cheek. It was a beautiful gesture, and I only hope I can bring myself to be as generous in defeat.

The Overall Individual results were:

1:	Nadia Comaneci	79·275
2:	Nelli Kim	78·675
3:	Ludmilla Tourischeva	78·625
4:	Teodora Ungureanu	78·375
5:	Olga Korbut	78·025

The Apparatus finals followed on Thursday; despite having the Overall Individual title under my belt I had no intention of letting up.

On the basis of the performances over the last few days, Bela had reckoned on the likely winners in the various disciplines being as follows: Nelli Kim on the vault, Tourischeva on the floor, and me on the bars and beam.

'Just carry on doing the same things and the medals will be yours.'

That was precisely what I had in mind.

The vault came first. I did not do well, failing to spot my piked Tsukahara, then following it with an almost equally weak second vault. My score was only 9·85. It was the same mark that helped Tourischeva to a joint silver with Carola Dombeck of the DDR, their scores being 19·650. Nelli won the vault gold with a score of 19·800.

Next came the bars. I received another ten points, which when added to my previous ten meant that I could not be caught. Dorina earned 9·90 and thereby the silver medal, with Marta Egervari picking up the bronze. Nelli wrecked her chances of a medal with an unfortunate fall from the bars.

The beam followed, and another score of ten came up against my name. The gold was mine. Both Olga and Dorina got a 9·90, with Olga eventually taking the silver and Teodora the bronze. It had been a very satisfying final for me by the time we came to the final discipline, the floor.

There was no way that I could overtake Nelli or Ludmilla, but I had a chance of taking the bronze. Nelli, in a very lively performance, scored the last perfect mark of the Games and in so doing just robbed Ludmilla of a much deserved gold. A 9·95 secured the bronze for me which, along with my other Olympic medals, has taken pride of place in my trophy cabinet.

With the end of the gymnastics events at the Olympics, my thoughts turned to the task of avoiding the barrage of attention from officials, TV and assorted dignitaries who had been taken by the success of the Romanian team. Bela, the Federation and Olympic Committee agreed that it would be best for all of us in the team if we were allowed home early, and weren't made to wait for the closing ceremony.

Two days before leaving Canada, Bela took us to Camp Robinson which was far removed from the hustle and bustle of the big city. There we put on a demonstration using some old rustic apparatus – wooden logs for beams, for example. We were still being carefully watched by Bela and Marta, but this impromptu display did give us the chance to meet and talk to some of the young children staying at camp. One thing I discovered at Camp Robinson was that my prowess at table-tennis leaves much to be desired.

We arrived back at Otopeni airport on July 27 to a tremendous welcome in fine weather. It was a tearful reunion with my family, I was overjoyed to be back. (The only sad note was that a fluffy toy rabbit that had been given to me at one of the Montreal press gatherings as a memento and of which I'd grown fond, was wrenched from me in the crowd at the airport.)

Before we could leave for a long summer holiday at a private beach on the Black Sea Coast, we were taken to the beautiful new Palace of Sport and Culture in the south of the city, where the team was honored in the presence of our President, Nicolae Ceausescu, and senior State officials, I felt very humble as I walked up to shake hands with the President. He awarded me the gold Medal of a Hero of Socialist Labor. I was very impressed by him, and most pleasantly surprised by his genuine interest and kindness. It was a moment I will never forget.

After the summer holidays were over, it was business as usual and we were soon back in training. At the same time, our Olympic success brought with it the obligation to meet dignitaries, visit sports institutes and generally endure a certain amount of celebrity treatment, all without letting our education or training slide.

The first competition scheduled after the Games was the Chunichi Cup in Nagoya, Japan. Just before that I was invited to a gymnastics display in Antibes. It is a beautiful place and I was given a chance to relax, as very little fuss was made. Princess Grace of Monaco was kind enough to present me with a beautiful little gold wristwatch which I wear to this day. Then, a few weeks later, we were off to Japan. With a score of 39·75 I managed to win the Cup, with Teodora hot on my heels with 39·05.

Contrary to what was being rumored in the press, I didn't find it at all difficult to stay motivated after the Olympics. People tended to assume that there was nothing left to aim for, having achieved a perfect score and Olympic victory before I was fifteen. In truth all that happened was that I had achieved "perfection" under a certain system, but there was plenty of room for developing that system and therefore gymnastics as a whole, and indeed the new Code of Points governing the sport has had the effect, among other things, of extending the boundaries of gymnastics so that a perfect score will be harder to achieve than ever.

12

SO IT'S back to Moscow, to the time when Nicolae Vieru and I were sitting together in the Village discussing the likely course of events in the Individual Apparatus Finals. Nicu was confident that we had seen the back of the worst excesses of partisan judging. I wished that I shared his confidence. Both Emilia and Melita were in with a chance of medals, as well as myself. Nicu was extremely pleased to see several Romanian girls so highly placed.

Although I had made it through to three of the four finals, the one that was most important to me, the asymmetric bars, was denied to me as a result of my fall in the earlier competition. This slip forced me to dredge my soul for the motivation to raise my morale again. The very fact that I was competing at the highest level helped me pull myself together. It wasn't so much that I didn't want to let the audience down, I knew what I was capable of, and whenever I fall below my own standards, I feel pretty sick with myself. To do so in front of the world only rubs salt into the wound.

The vault final was a bit of an anti-climax really. Only Natalia Shaposhnikova was awarded the kind of marks that had been regularly earned in previous rounds. Her best vault was given a score of 9·825 which, when added to her 9·90 carried over from earlier rounds, gave her the winning score of 19·725. The rest of us were certainly not doing our best, and I was one of the worst offenders. After bringing forward marks of 9·95 and 9·90, I slumped, almost literally, to 9·425 in the final round, and finished second to last. While the judging was generally more strict than it had been earlier in the competition, mine was a pretty dismal display of vaulting. Going into the last round, Maxi, Steffi, and myself were leading with identical scores of 19·850. Both Natalia Shaposhnikova and Melita Ruhn had notched up perfect marks, Natalia for her set (compulsory) vault and Melita for her voluntary one. The medal placings were:

113

1: Natalia Shaposhnikova (USSR)   19·725
2: Steffi Kraker (DDR)   19·675
3: Melita Ruhn (Romania)   19·650

They deserved the medals because they proved the most consistent performers, and I was delighted that Melita earned a bronze, which helped to remove some of my own disappointment.

The bars competition was of much higher standard, though I found it terribly frustrating to watch. I kept wanting to jump up and show everybody that my earlier lapse was just a freak. Both Maxi and Emilia had gotten maximum points in their voluntaries in the team event during the first stage of the Games (the team event is in two parts – the sets and the voluntaries). For Competition III (the Individual Apparatus Finals) the scores from Competition 1a and Competition 1b, the Team Finals, are added together, then divided by two and added to the marks given for the Apparatus Final to determine the final positions. It sounds complicated! but you get used to it. . . Remarkably, with the exception of Nelli who'd scored 9·85, all the other girls got 9·90. These were the medalists:

    1: Maxi Gnauck (DDR)   19·875
    2: Emilia Eberle (Romania)   19·850
  =3: Melita Ruhn (Romania)   19·775
  =3: Steffi Kraker (DDR)   19·775
  =3: Maria Filatova (USSR)   19.775

Bela was delighted at the successes of two members of his squad, and Romania still had an interest in the two remaining pieces of apparatus.

Now came the balance beam – my earlier performance having placed me in the lead. It was Shaposhnikova that I wanted to keep a close eye on, because if I were to make a mistake she could prove a serious threat. However, I felt quietly confident about this discipline. I thought Elena Davydova's score of 9·90 was very high, considering that she wobbled a couple of times. Bela obviously thought so too as he looked across to me as if to say, 'here we go again'.

I also thought that the judges had been a bit unfair to Natalia, as I felt she'd put in a better performance than Elena – but she received 9·85. It was the same score that I was given. That particular number had been etched into my brain after the fiasco of the previous competition, but this time I felt very different about the outcome, for the gold was mine.

    1: Nadia Comaneci (Romania)   19·800
    2: Elena Davydova (USSR)   19·750
    3: Natalia Shaposhnikova (USSR) 19·725

It was a sweet victory which Bela rewarded with one of his bearlike hugs. Even I felt a little emotional when, standing on the rostrum with the gold around my neck, the Romanian flag was hoisted aloft. Flanked by two Soviet flags, the symbolism of the struggle at the Moscow Games was not lost on me, nor I suspect, those watching on TV back in Romania. Mind you, there was very little time to be reflective, for there was another final to come.

The floor final was going to be very tough indeed. As things stood there were four of us tying for first place. Nelli, Natalia, Maxi, and myself all had a carry over score of 9·925. However, in the dying moments of a competitive program, tiredness can often cause you to make mistakes, and it seemed unlikely that any of us would put in a truly magnificent performance. As it turned out, some pretty peculiar judging did its bit to allocate the final medal.

Maxi and Natalia both put in exemplary performances, which earned them 9·90 apiece. Emilia also worked very well, finishing with a spritely tumbling sequence for a 9·85. Nelli's familiar floor-music started, and off she went. However, during the course of her exercise, she nearly fell at the end of two of her tumbling routines. Perhaps understandably after a long week's competition, her exercise looked a little leaden footed. I could see that she was breathing heavily when she dismounted the raised floor area. When her mark of 9·95 came up, I was shocked. I wasn't the only one; for Maxi and her coach stared in amazement at the score. Bela suggested tersely that Nelli was being handed a retirement present.

Anyway, my turn came, the cassette music blared out from the huge speakers, and I began my last Olympic performance, I had summoned all my strength in a final desperate attempt to secure a gold medal; it was all or nothing.

When the score came up, I found that the effort had not been enough – I was in silver position. But when I noticed yet another judges' conference starting up, I couldn't believe it. Surely, the Moscow gymnastics competition wasn't going to end on a sour note after all the problems that had occurred earlier. However, it transpired that there had been a machine failure on the electronic scoring machine, and that one of the judge's scores had been wrongly posted. A check of the scoring slips that all panel members have to complete confirmed the error and the result of the final was amended accordingly.

=1: Nelli Kim (USSR)   19·875
=1: Nadia Comaneci (Romania)   19·875
=3: Maxi Gnauck (DDR)   19·825
=3: Natalia Shaposhnikova (USSR) 19·825

I was physically and mentally exhausted, despite my elation at having won a second gold at the Games. The whole week had been grueling and now all that I wanted to do was get home as quickly as possible.

Back in our apartment, it was at last possible to relax and forget about gymnastics. Dana Turner and I just collapsed on to our beds and with a heartfelt, 'Thank God it's all over,' fell into a deep sleep. Food, for once, could wait until later. We were woken by Nicu who explained that there was going to be a press conference, after which we would be leaving early to return home. The news of our early return fortified me for the press conference, which turned out to be a cinch compared to the circus four years earlier at Montreal. Perhaps the Soviet press were less taken with Romanian gymnastics!

We slipped quietly out of the Olympic Village for the journey to Sheremetievo Airport and thence to Bucharest. Looking back at the apartment buildings, I couldn't help wondering what sort of people would be living in our apartment when the Games were over and the facilities handed over to the people of Moscow.

I sat next to Dana on the flight home; all we could think about was seeing our families, and then a long hot summer spent walking in the mountains and soaking up the sun on the beaches by the Black Sea. Emil Draganescu, our Minister for Sport and Tourism, met us off the plane, and his cheerful face was the perfect welcome home. My family was there to greet me, and we left directly for Deva. The reception that we got when we arrived was lovely. Although I had not been training at Deva for three months before the Olympics, there were many familiar faces and I was showered with congratulations and kisses. It was marvelous to be among so many good friends again.

After a short stay in the mountains around Poiana Brasov, a superb ski resort in winter, we were off to the coast. Here I was free to indulge myself swimming, dancing, and eating ice-cream. Provided that I took some exercise every day, I was free to eat what I liked when I liked. It was a nice change from those times when Bela or Marta watched my eating habits like hawks. I well remember a squall that blew up in England about three weeks before the Fort Worth World Championships in 1979.

We had just left Frankfurt and traveled to Huddersfield, an industrial town in the north of England, where we were due to compete against the British national team. I had serious problems with sciatica which prevented me from participating, so my time was very much my own. In fact, I was rather bored, being obliged to sit on the sidelines while my teammates got on with the competition.

After the first evening, we had our usual meager dinner in the hotel restaurant, under the curious eyes of the British team. Although I was allowed to eat more food than my companions, as I no longer had a problem with my weight, my meal was still not what you could call a feast. I was rooming with Marilena Vladarau and, at about nine o'clock in the evening, we ordered some sandwiches to be sent up. Just our luck! As they were brought to our door, who should happen to be passing but Bela? He hit the roof and sent the waitress away. When Bela loses his temper, mountains tumble. We had a good old fashioned slanging match inside the room. Marilena just sat on the bed and let Bela and me get on with it. It was a long and hungry night that followed.

The next day was the last of the competition, after which followed the official reception. While all the usual speeches were being made Bela and I left the room to get some food from the buffet area. Bela watched as I piled a plate high with trifle. Then I spotted some of my favorite cakes – chocolate éclairs, and looked across imploringly at Bela. 'Go on then, take a couple. I don't mind you eating like this so long as the others don't see. They don't understand that they can't be allowed to eat freely yet. They will see it as favoritism, which would be bad for team discipline. That's why I was so angry last night. You were leading Marilena astray.'

I took three éclairs and put them in with the trifle, while Bela laughed at my antics with the lady serving behind the tables. It was a delicious way to survive yet another official reception, and indulge a craving for sweet things. Mind you, most of the girls are just as bad, and I have visions of today's entire generation of girl gymnasts ending up as tomorrow's weightwatchers! Gheorghe Gorgoi, my new coach, does not object to Anca and myself indulging ourselves – but if he catches us passing any goodies to the others, we're in trouble.

When I returned to Bucharest on September 8 to resume my training with Gheorghe Gorgoi, and also with Anca, now that she is a Professor of Sport and has stopped competing, there were several other important aspects of my future to think about. Priority number one was to pass entrance exams into the University so that I could also study to become a coach. This meant I had to bring schoolbooks into the training hall, as well as having extra tutorials in Biology. My sporting commitments mean that the amount of time available for studying is severely limited, but somehow I still need to make the time for a proper education. Any person with such commitments is bound to be at a serious disadvantage when it comes to sitting exams. Cramming becomes the order of the day. There are only ever about forty places available on the coaching course and there are usually about three hundred applicants. It is highly competitive, but as I am sure you have guessed by now, one thing I enjoy is a good challenge.

Combining studies with training requires almost superhuman self-discipline at times. I was futher distracted by the fact that I was looking for a new home, and I was also desperate to take my driving test.

I finished the exams and physical tests on October 23, 1980 and managed to come seventh out of all the applicants. Now at last, I knew where I was going. In the meantime, a house had been located near the Republicii Stadium that was suitable for my mother, brother, and I to move into over the Christmas period. It is a beautiful old house on the corner of a very quiet street and has four levels to it. There is a large cellar, a ground floor, first floor, and an enormous attic, which I've already earmarked for a disco. It is great to feel settled at last. Adrian is happy studying at his new school, and is spending every free minute practicing his tennis. He has already made his mark on the house by breaking one of the windows in the hall while trying to improve his backhand, and threatens to become the new Ilie Nastase in a few years time.

It will take us a good year to get the place sorted out. Although I am very interested in decorating, other things will no doubt take priority. I'd love to put on some old clothes and get myself covered in various shades of paint, perhaps throw a wallpapering party or two, but I doubt I'll get the time. Still, my new home represents a sanctuary. I think of it as a place I can retreat to whenever the pressures of being Nadia Comaneci start getting a bit heavy and as a place from which I intend to strike out for new goals.

Talking of goals, one that I have managed to achieve most recently is to be let loose in the driving seat of a car. Ever since we came to live in Bucharest, I have found myself being driven around the city by Anca. She has a bright red Lada, and if red is a warning color, then other drivers seem to take the hint, because whenever they see Anca's in their driving mirrors, they invariably move over. This is not a typical way for Romanian drivers to behave: perhaps they can sense the passion with which she drives. Mind you, there are times when I think she would be better suited to rally driving!

With such an example, it was not surprising that I should develop a strong desire to taste the freedom of the open road. The driving school was perfectly located for me, being right at the back of our sports complex.

I very nearly missed my driving test though, because I found myself stuck in hospital at that time. It had been decided that my appendix should be removed as soon as a slack period in my training schedule arose. At the time it was more of a preventive measure than anything else. The appendix had become severely inflamed just before the Moscow Games, and doctors advised me that I shouldn't go, but should have an operation immediately. However, the appendix calmed down just in time and I was given the all clear for the Olympics on the understanding that it would come out at the earliest opportunity on my return.

Looking back on my gymnastic's career, I have been remarkably fortunate with my health. When I think about some of the broken limbs that some of my fellow competitors have suffered, I count my blessings. My worst legacy is the disc compression in my spine that causes the pain along the sciatic nerve, but that is inconvenient rather than serious. There is also a scar left by the operation in Fort Worth's All Saints Hospital to drain a cellulitis infection in my left wrist. But apart from these, all I have had to cope with so far is a few sprains in my wrists and ankles and the occasional inflamed tendon. Whether there will be any delayed reaction to the stress imposed on the body by modern gymnastics is something only time will reveal.

Speculation persists that I am considering retirement because my body cannot keep up with the demands made upon it. The truth is that I hope to have a few more seasons at the top of my sport; I also like to think that my more recent performances have branded the rumors that I am finished as a top-class competitor as a little premature. In fact, as long as I keep enjoying the sport and coping with the discipline that it demands I shall continue. With Anca and Gheorghe Gorgoi coaching us, it is a very happy squad that trains at the 23rd August Park. Sadly though we have recently lost the company of Gabi Gheorghiu – but then Adina Farcuts has returned to us (she trained with me when I was first in Bucharest in '78). Teodora Ungureanu has recently retired from gymnastics to start a family after marrying Sorin Cepoi, one of our male gymnasts, at the beginning of 1981. Her heart had not been in gymnastics for some time and most of us knew where her heart really lay.

Today the hardest task facing an upcoming competitive gymnast is finding original elements and combinations for his or her exercises. This is a problem I also have to contend with more and more. Originality is essential to earn the bonus points necessary to maximize your score. All of the top competitiors strive for these so-called ROV points (it stands for Risk, Originality, and Virtuosity) and need them if they are to stand any chance of winning medals in major competitions. Unless the rules or the equipment are changed soon, gymnastics will be reaching a state of stagnation in a few years' time as there won't be any new ideas left. The whole system is already due for a rethink. Although I have managed to find one or two new moves to include in my new exercises, I don't know where the next lot are going to come from.

13

HAVING BEEN given the opportunity of looking back over my career so far – I can't think of this book as an autobiography in any real sense – I have come to some firm conclusions about my sport. Some readers might like to know where I, as a competitive gymnast, stand on many of the issues facing the sport today. So, I'll take a deep breath and voice my opinions.

One thing I have noticed is that it seems to be fashionable for pundits to take a hefty swipe at modern gymnastics, mostly in connexion with the women's event. Funnily enough, for they were the dominant side of the sport until the late Sixties, the men are considered the "poor relations" of the sport today. The greater popularity of the women is a recent, and largely Western, phenomenon. Young women gymnasts seem to have a far greater appeal, especially to television audiences and, I feel, we get a far larger amount of media interest than we truly deserve.

Let me say straight away that on the whole I feel very positive about the future of gymnastics. If I'd felt otherwise, I would have left the sport before now. The areas that appear to give rise to the greatest concern are, firstly, the physical and psychological pressures placed on the young female gymnast, and secondly, the fact that a political or nationalistic bias seems to have intruded into much of the judging at international level. There is obviously some justification for worry on both counts, but I can't help feeling that the press have, at times, been guilty of painting a more depressing picture than the sport deserves.

As for the psychological strain under which young gymnasts have to work these days, it only really applies to those at the highest levels of sport. Pressure is a part of the game for all top athletes, in all sports, as it is for people at the top in any walk of life; this is nothing exclusive to women's gymnastics. But the bodies that govern the sport have a special duty of care in the case of women's gymnastics because the average age of today's competitors is considerably lower than that for any other sports, with the possible exception of swimming and ice-skating. In part, women's gymnastics seems to be just a reflection of a growing trend in sports towards what is called "cult of youth" – just look at what is happening in women's tennis nowadays. I don't believe that, as a general rule, young people are unable to take pressure; on the contrary, I think on the whole they are remarkably resilient, and in most cases enjoy a challenge. From an early age, children everywhere are confronted by challenges and a certain amount of pressure: to do well at school, to pass exams that could affect a whole career, and so on. The pressures we are talking about are not, in any case, negative; motivation, dedication, self-discipline and self-denial are all qualities that are generally admired.

There is nothing wrong with children being encouraged to develop skills and talents – it is only when they are forced into something, whether out of motives of nationalistic or parental ambition, that we should worry, and I have never met a gymnast who had to be forced to compete! Admittedly, there were times when I felt overpowered by my former coach, Bela, but that is a pretty common reaction by a young pupil to a teacher, and I didn't appreciate the results his rigid training system would bring about. Besides, most amateur sports authorities are conscientious and have built-in checks to stop abuse.

Certainly, the increased popularity of my sport has brought with it increasing pressure to succeed, which is felt by all top competitors, but this is something which is part of the evolution of every sport. The motivation for success still has to come from within each individual. You can impose discipline, but you can't impose success. Although we are taught not to accept failure, it is something all of us have to face from time to time and, I am convinced, we are better people for having learned to suffer defeat.

Success in any sport, and I suppose in life itself, is all about confidence; recognize your limitations by all means, but work away at trying to push them further back all the time. It is unbelievable what can be achieved if you only try. Aim for the impossible. Failure is always easiest to bear when you know in yourself that you have given your best, and maybe a little extra.

The physical stresses which have to be endured by women gymnasts today are immense. I can't pretend I have always found it easy to keep to such a strict routine of diet and exercise. But there is no easy route to gaining complete control over your body when aiming for perfection of movement. Sports such as ice-skating and diving make similar

122

demands on the performer, as they too rely as much on aesthetic appeal as on technical virtuosity.

Gymnastics is undoubtedly more technically complex than ever before. The number of times that the same moves or sequences have to be repeated in training and in the competition hall is frightening, but it is vital to get as close as possible to a position where you can perform your routine almost instinctively.

This subject aroused a lot of interest around the time of the 1976 Olympics, and Bela was asked at Montreal to estimate how often I had rehearsed the flic-flac on the beam; he replied that I had probably executed it about 20,000 times. That is a mind-boggling figure, but probably a little conservative, and it only covered the period up to and including the Games in '76. I don't even want to think what that figure would be now. The flic-flac is also one of the least difficult or demanding movements. Practicing forward or backward somersaults on the beam from a standing position is certainly harder work, yet these are now common elements in every gymnast's repertoire.

Recent evidence has shown that modern gymnastics does put a young girl at risk – it can cause damage to a developing body if it is subjected to the same routine as the seniors. Usually the youngsters only spend about half as much time on the apparatus as their elders. The joints take the greatest pounding, and some years back several gymnastics countries found that a large proportion of their young girl athletes began to suffer from arthritic conditions. In Romania, the youngster, or *mica gimnasta* as she is called, spends a lot of her early days in the gymnasium playing on the apparatus to prepare herself for the rigors of taking the sport seriously. This allows her body to become familiar with the equipment in its own good time and prevents problems later in life. I suppose I am living proof of this.

Then of course, there is the element of physical risk associated with some of the more complex gymnastic moves. A degree of risk is inherent in most sports and if a ban was placed on every sport that endangers life and limb, there wouldn't be many left. All that can be done is to try and prevent any unnecessary risk creeping into the sport. The new Code of Points was created with a view to keeping the escalation of risk elements in the various exercises in check, but it does not yet seem to have succeeded in this aim. The quest for those precious ROV bonus points has continued to oblige competitors to take more risks.

Elena Mukhina's (the Soviet former world champion) tragic accident was the result of her failing to complete one of those dangerous elements. The same move had previously killed one of the male gymnasts in a Balkan championship. Kamikaze tactics should not be part of gymnastics.

The whole question of judging is very difficult. Yes, there is undoubted national and political interference with the system; this is almost inevitable when international judging panels are made up of and supervised by officials and ex-competitors from the countries that dominate the sport. But most of the time, I feel that the problem is much more basic. The judges simply don't know how to judge! Traveling around the world, I have noticed that some of the marking often amazes both competitors and coaches alike; and not just when it's their turn. Judging anything is a difficult and inexact art, but it's a pity when bizarre marking threatens to make a complete nonsense of all of the hard work we have put in. I hate to be given more marks than I know I deserve just as much as I dislike feeling I've been marked down.

However I realize that the whole matter is still very subjective. The Code of Points is certainly tighter than it used to be but, as we have seen, serious disputes still occur.

One of the other things I find unhealthy about gymnastics is the large gap between the top five countries and the rest of the competing nations. As is quite common in sports, the outcome of major events are sometimes too predictable for gymnastics' own good, though the gap between countries seems to be closing nowadays and I hope that all of us who love the sport will be in for a few surprises in the coming years.

There can be no doubt that coaches form the backbone of gymnastics. They have a heavy responsibility. In the well run Federations, they are the people who put together national training programs, lobby for facilities, and encourage an interest in the sport at an early age. On top of all this, they must also coach their squad for five or six days of every week.

In Romania, all of our coaches are highly qualified, as it takes several years of study and practise before a would-be coach is ready to sit the exams. A coach has to be highly qualified not only technically, but in his or her ability to respond to being placed in a position of great trust. When that coach is dealing with young children, and is likely to be with them for some years, he or she inevitably becomes something of a surrogate parent. Bad coaching, in the fullest sense, can wreck more than a child's gymnastics, for it can have a lasting effect on a child's personality.

So what makes a coach? There's no such thing as a perfect coach because the trainer who is right for one gymnast may be quite wrong for others. Personality and temperament play an important role in the relationship between any teacher and pupil, and these are always two-edged swords. In Romania we have teams of coaches in the schools which allow every child a chance to train under the person who suits them best. A coach must genuinely care for his pupils, but must also be prepared to be cruel to be kind. It can be painful to watch if tears start flowing. But usually, once the lesson is over, the coach will take the child, or sometimes the adult, aside to emphasize that tough talking is a natural part of the training process.

One good thing that has happened over the last few years is that there are more women getting involved in coaching gymnastics. It has taken a long time for this to happen – but better late than never. I love seeing someone like Ludmilla Tourischeva in charge of a team. I firmly believe that all of us who have enjoyed participating in the sport should be encouraged to re-invest our experience and enthusiasm.

And where does my own future lie? Well, I am not foolish enough to think that I can compete successfully for much longer. As long as I enjoy gymnastics and feel that I can represent my country and my sport with honor, I'll continue. But I have earned a rest, and look forward to being able to put my feet up just a little when the time comes. There are few ambitions, in competitive terms, that I have left to fulfill.

I definitely want to stay involved with gymnastics and that is why I am studying to become a coach. I would also like to become a judge of international standard. Quite by chance Anca and I seem to have chosen identical plans for the future. One day, I would like to be in charge of the Romanian Gymnastics Federation, but that is a year or two away yet! Actually I don't think my temperament is suited to sitting behind a desk. But time will tell.

I know that Anca feels she can never train junior gymnasts, because she loves youngsters too much to be able to be very strict with them. I feel pretty much the same way, so I suspect that I will choose to coach older competitiors.

Before then I still have my University course to complete. One of the good things about my sport is that it is in a state of constant development, throwing up new challenges and ideas to inspire a lifetime's devotion. I hope that once I stop competing I will still be able to contribute to it and to keep in touch with the many friends I have made on my overseas trips. Sometimes I regret that I have not been able to spend enough time getting to know the worldwide gymnastics fraternity – perhaps that is something for the future. But that doesn't mean I don't realize how lucky I am, for not many young people get the opportunity to travel the world, while "working" at something that they love.

I owe a great deal to my country, for allowing me to pursue my chosen sport. I have worked very hard for my achievements, but without the enthusiasm and support of a dedicated gymnastics adminstration it's quite likely my talents would have gone unfulfilled. That, sadly is all too common. Through all the experiences that have been part of my sports career, I have been able to learn a lot about myself, including the fact that I'm not nearly as cool and unflappable as many people including yours truly tend to believe. Deep down, I suppose, I am as sensitive and vulnerable as the next girl, or the next human being perhaps I should say.

All in all, I suppose that I do quite like myself after all. The intense, introspective yet passionate young girl who caused her parents so much despair a few years ago has probably been responsible for much of my success. Of course, my life is really just beginning, but I like to think that my years as a competitive gymnast have been a useful grounding for it.

Appendices

Nadia: an assessment

by Graham Buxton Smither

I WAS asked to assess Nadia Comaneci's place in the history of gymnastics and while at first it seemed a daunting prospect, it is a subject which interests me greatly and one to which I have devoted a lot of thought over the last few years. I was also asked, as a close friend of Nadia's, to give an insight into her character to determine how certain qualities have helped her to the top. For the sake of our friendship I hope the lady finds nothing here that will surprise, shock or annoy!

To determine the significance of Nadia's contribution to gymnastics, it's necessary to know something about recent developments in the sport and to place her achievements in their historical context. It is also important to decide which factors should form the basis of our critical appraisal. Obviously, her medal successes at major competitions will give a useful indication of her competitive ability, but surely there is a lot more to be considered here than a mere balance-sheet of medals. This takes no account, for example of the actual content of the exercises or the artistic merit of a particular performance. All the various elements of Nadia's work need therefore to be carefully weighed against her rivals' performances in order to compose an unofficial list of "all time greats". Then there is also the question of how Nadia may have changed the nature of the sport to be decided.

The history of women's gymnastics – the individual overall and apparatus finals – only began at the Helsinki Olympic games in 1952. In the thirty odd years since women's gymnastics has been represented at this level there have been many great women gymnasts but only a few that can be described as truly outstanding. In terms of medals won at Olympic events, Latynina, Caslavska and Comaneci head the list. If European and World Championships are to be included, then Tourischeva and Kim must be added. However, as I've already indicated, I find this to be a very shallow way of deciding their respective

131

merits and their influence on the sport. Such a list would exclude Korbut who, whilst obviously not the greatest in terms of sheer technique, has had a lasting influence on the artistic interpretation of the exercises.

It is important to be aware that technically, gymnastics has become far more complex over the last 10 years or so, the degree of difficulty necessary in modern exercises surpassing anything that could have been visualized in the late fifties and sixties. An examination of the beam or bars medal winning routines of Caslavska and Comaneci during their respective Olympics, reveals the enormous disparity in the degree of difficulty that has developed. Ignoring, for the moment, the beautiful artistic interpretation of Vera Caslavska, the content of her exercises would be too simple by modern standards for even a junior gymnast to perform with any expectation of success at a major competition. However, this should in no way detract from the esteem in which she is still held because, in her day, her work was innovatory and of the highest quality that was then considered attainable.

However, the fact that modern competitors could perform Caslavska's routines with consummate ease is not entirely a reflection on today's higher technical demands, but is also related to the difference in physique of the top competitors nowadays. In the days of Latynina, Caslavska and Tourischeva, the women were more mature than the successful youngsters of today. Physically, these older gymnasts, being taller and heavier, would find if difficult to execute some of the more complex elements that are essential now. Both Latynina and Caslavska were twenty-two when they scored their first real successes at the Olympics. Nadia was fourteen and half when she became Overall Olympic Champion at Montreal.

Thus, on technical ability, Nadia scores over the other great names. Nadia was the first to receive a perfect score, and this was repeated at the Montreal Games on no less than seven occasions. She had made Olympic and gymnastic history, and many subsequent "10's" have proved that this was no freak occurence. Even amidst the controversies of the 1980 Olympics, few who witnessed her second bars voluntary exercise will ever forget the sheer technical supremacy she displayed and the "10" she was subsequently awarded. She and her colleagues in the Romanian Team have been great innovators, both of specific elements like the Comaneci somersault and dismount, but also, perhaps unwittingly, of the current style of the sport which favors risk and technical complexity.

If there has been one recurrent criticism of Nadia in the past, it has concerned the expressive and artistic merits of her performances. For when Nadia first appeared on the international scene at the age of thirteen, she was very different from the two leading women gymnasts – namely the graceful, almost balletic, Tourischeva and the vivacious Korbut. Until Nadia's emergence, Olga Korbut was thought to represent all that was new in gymnastics and she was clearly the darling of the public. In their minds, it boiled down to a contest between "Korbut the Clown" and "Comaneci the Computer"; for, by comparison with Olga, Nadia was unresponsive and unexpressive almost, her critics felt, to the point of inhumanity. Watching her floor work left one feeling slightly uneasy; all the elements and combinations were there but the verve and spontaneous enjoyment of a Korbut were missing. Nadia was, however, only thirteen years old at that time and as she has grown, both physically and emotionally, her artistic interpretation has improved enormously and this is reflected in all the areas of her performance. It was no accident that she finally won a floor gold medal at the Moscow Olympics, in 1980.

When the results of the European Championships are taken into account, Nadia has a unique place once again. She now has the European Trophy to herself, having won the overall title on three consecutive occasions; in 1975, 1977, and 1979. It should be remembered that she went through a traumatic physical change during these years as she developed from a child into a woman, and yet she was able to continue improving her content and style and maintain a consistency of form that confounded her critics. It was by any standards a remarkable achievement.

Yet, by contrast, the one competition that she has failed to make any real impression upon has been the World Championships. In Strasbourg at the 1978 Championships, she was at the most difficult stage of her physical transformation, and was not prepared for the task of competing. She still managed to win an individual apparatus gold, and a silver medal, but, by her own high standards, she had failed. Sadly, at the next World Championships in Fort Worth, 1979, she had to retire from the event due to a serious infection in her wrist that required an immediate operation. She was leading the competition prior to her withdrawal, but by way of consolation, the Romanian Team deposed the Soviet Union and took the gold medal, and Nadia had a team gold to return home with. It could be said that the timing of the two World Championships, since she started competing internationally, has been far from kind to her.

These days there are more events around the world that are attended by the top gymnasts than in the sixties, and the level of competition is much higher and tougher. The pressure this puts on the top women

133

gymnasts is considerable, for it must be remembered that in order merely to maintain a previous mark in a later competition, under the new Code of Points a competitor must raise the content of her exercises and seek new elements and combinations. Although this is the case for everyone, if, as so often in Nadia's case, you start out with a perfect score, the pressure to equal it is far greater than if you were going from 9·90 to 9·95, because it is the "10's" that are most remembered.

So what of her influence on the sport? Well, Olga Korbut was without doubt the biggest influence in the early seventies as a result of her televized performances at the Munich Olympics. Her irrepressible personality and tiny child-like frame won the hearts of millions. Within one year of her Munich debut, many others were trying to find gymnasts built along her lines who were also able to play to the auditorium. The era of the gamine had arrived.

What are the personal qualities that have made Nadia such a marvelous sportswoman? For a start, she has a body that is a coach's dream – it appears to have been tailor-made for the sport. She is slender, supple, long limbed, has narrow hips, natural speed and strength. It goes without saying that she has a perfect sense of balance. These qualities are to be found in many of the best gymnasts, but few have been so successful at using them to their full advantage and I think, therefore, that the difference lies in the personality and psychological make-up of Nadia. For the moment, I will concern myself only with those characteristics that apply directly to her sport.

Nadia is one of the most wilful people that I have ever encountered, and in sport most of the great names have strong wills. Trying to dissuade her from a path upon which she has set her mind is an exhausting and often futile exercise. It is this single-minded dedication that is undoubtedly responsible for her success. Gymnastics is the sport that she loves, but it demands total commitment of its disciples. She is, by any standards a remarkable person, and when she chose to reject the simple pleasures of a normal childhood, it revealed a powerful competitive instinct. However, she never seems to be aware of competing against others, the competition is always against herself and her own limitations. Self-discipline was instilled in her at a very early stage by her former coaches, in particular Bela Karoly, and she has managed to retain self-control despite being able to sample the greater freedoms of a more adult environment. Recently she has shown remarkable iron will in deciding the amount of relaxation she can afford to allow herself: an excess one day will be balanced by abstinence the next.

Being with her in training is most instructive and all the traits mentioned above can be seen to good effect. When the coach leaves the hall, (usually for a quick smoke) the others will often slacken off or stop training altogether but not Nadia – she knows the value of training and will work until she feels that she has done as much as she's capable of. She is the only member of her squad who can decide for herself how much to train, or even if to train on a particular day. She is trusted to know what is best for her.

She has the particularly interesting ability of being able to construct and visualize movements, without recourse to written diagrams. This means she has the extraordinary talent of being able to create new movements in her mind without having to try them out first in the gym. She has a thorough comprehension of the mechanics of gymnastics and this will be invaluable when she turns her talents to coaching.

There have been times however, when, although her mind has told her that she could make a particular movement, her body has failed to respond. At this point others would resign themselves to failure and try again the next day. Not so with Nadia, her face hardens, her eyes burn with anger, and all that fury is directed at the offending piece of apparatus until she gets it right, and can repeat it.

But what of Nadia the person? What are her good points, and bad ones? Just what kind of person is she?

She is one of the most complicated people to try to assess. There is a strange magic about this young lady that her few close friends all agree upon. She can, however, be very elusive – which can be rather off-putting at first. For example if she asks a question which requires detailed explanation, she often appears not to be listening to the answer – her thoughts seem to be miles away. At first, I took this to indicate either simple bad manners or an inability to assimilate complex information. It was not to be the last occasion on which I was to misjudge her. For a later conversation revealed that she had absorbed everything I had said, and that she had formed her own ideas on the subject. Even so, this tendency of drifting away in conversation is very often an indication of boredom. One of Nadia's problems is that she is easily bored; unless the subject captures her imagination or is of vital importance, she tends to tire of it very quickly. She is not a particularly patient person.

At first sight Nadia seemed like another Korbut carbon-copy, although no one could continue to hold this opinion once they'd see her perform. Here was a very serious-minded young girl who appeared to be dedicated to the pursuit of perfection. She seemed oblivious to the spectators' applause, the apparatus being all that she saw, all that she responded to. No one could deny that she was a singularly unusual gymnast, combining the suppleness, agility, and courage of youth with the dedication and discipline of an adult. There were never any histrionics from this young lady and many people were frightened that she had somehow been dehumanized in the interest of the sport. What Nadia had done was to surrender, by her own wishes, her childhood to devote herself to her favorite pastime – gymnastics. What she achieved was perfection, something which was previously thought to be unattainable. It was a barrier, rather like that of the four minute mile some time ago, which she and her coaches felt could be broken and therefore had to be broken.

Many coaches attempted to copy Nadia's style and suddenly there was a whole army of young, dynamic gymnasts demonstrating technical virtuosity above all else. This has led to a greater understanding of bio-mechanics which has in turn allowed far more complex and riskful movements to be attempted. Thus we can see that while Olga was responsible for the increase in popularity and participation in gymnastics, Nadia has in the same way been the inspiration behind the general raising of standards. Her new elegance, now that she is older, is winning admirers amongst the traditionalists, to whom as a child she was merely precocious. They see in the likes of Nadia and Nelli Kim a sign that the older, more physically developed, gymnast could well be coming back into fashion. The recent raising of the age level at which you can compete in Olympic events is also a step in this direction.

When her mind is not otherwise occupied, she watches everything and everyone. This is very noticeable at a competition, when, during the early part she can be seen assessing all her opponents, something she does quickly. She notes people's mannerisms and is a great mimic. It is a surprise to many that she has a great sense of humor, and is something of a practical joker. I remember that I was once leaving a hotel restaurant to go upstairs, precariously balancing a bottle and a couple of rolls on the way to the elevator, when halfway across the lobby, two unexpected digs in the ribs nearly propelled me into some pot plants!

It does not matter what is happening, whenever Nadia joins any group of people she quickly becomes the center of attention. Things naturally tend to revolve around her, whether at home, with friends, or in the gymnasium. But she is not at her most relaxed in a large group, especially when she is the center of attention. She is happiest with a small number of close friends whether she is at home, or out driving. The time when she most enjoys being part of a large gathering is in a discotheque surrounded by young people, who are more intent on dancing than seeing who else is on the floor.

Despite her considerable intelligence, Nadia is not an academic at heart. When I first went to Romania to see her, I had been told to expect a dull, machine-like, unintelligent, sullen and shy person. Only the latter is true, for she is a shy and private young lady. Yet it was Nadia who broke the ice on our first encounter, speaking in flawless English. It was to prove the first of many preconceptions that were to be destroyed. She has an alert, lively, and inquisitive mind, though as was said earlier, she can be impatient. She prefers the practical to the theoretical.

Her direct manner will never make her a diplomat, but she has learned to hold her tongue. Her often impassive features belie a deep sensitivity that is easily hurt. She has a warm, compassionate and caring nature that is not apparent in public. She enjoys the simple pleasures of life, measuring things in terms of personal happiness, not personal wealth. She is a patriot, and loves the beauty of her own country. While she enjoys traveling around the world, she is never happier than when she returns home to her family.

So how should Nadia be summed up? In gymnastics, she is without doubt the finest technician that the world has witnessed to date. Her historical record at the Montreal Olympics is unlikely to be equalled, let alone bettered. Her artistic interpretation has improved enormously, and there is now no obvious weakness in her repertoire. Arguably, her greatest contribution has been through her example, forcing everyone to raise their standards and aim for what was once thought unattainable. Even when she leaves the arena as a competitor, she is likely to return as a coach or a judge. Her love of her sport will continue to demand the best from her, and she will coax it out of her gymnasts. Nadia will not desert gymnastics.

Nadia's Horoscope

YOU WERE born with the sun in Scorpio and the moon in Capricorn which means that you have a somewhat hard, ambitious nature which can be a source of conflict in your life, as it can sometimes put you at variance with family, friends and the public. However, there are indications of high attainments; you remain steadfast and reliable when others with less determination fail. You are exacting in what you expect of others, but you make equally stern demands of yourself.

You are somewhat of an enigma to observers as you are often gloomy and indulge in brooding. If as a child you were in some way repressed by authority, you tended to overreact in a rather capricious, wilful manner. You do not easily enter into relationships, for you tend to think the worst of human nature.

You also have a sensitive and thoughtful disposition. You absorb information almost greedily and have a highly developed intelligence and memory. Generally fascinated by anything that arouses your curiosity, you are not satisfied until you have explored it thoroughly. Early in life you invented games or indoor activities which tested your ability to meet challenging competition. These mental-physical workouts prepared you for later confrontations with more serious opponents.

You project yourself amazingly well; young people are especially impressed with you and may even regard you as an example to aspire to. However, recognition is not as important to you as having the opportunity to fully utilize your talents.

When attracted to someone, your feelings are intense. You have a strong sexual desire but will always be best satisfied with someone with whom you have an intellectual rapport. You have great depth of understanding and the capacity to teach others what you have learned. You are modest and aware of your limitations but you also know how to make the most of your potential. Because you rarely voice an opinion unless asked, your views are considered authoritative and sincere.

Although you have an overriding ambition to succeed, you methodically plan each step towards your goals quietly and without fanfare, extracting important lessons from your experiences.

You are highly creative and may find expression either in socially orientated activities or in artistic pursuits. Occupations involving children and teaching seem particularly well suited. Your sense of drama would add excitement to learning. You are detached enough to be objective and, at the same time, emotional enough to be sensitive. You would strive to merit the trust others have given you.

You are not overly preoccupied with money, but consider it merely as a means of satisfying your most sincere objectives. You can be impatient and before you begin to try anything new you must be assured that the effort will not be wasted. Try not to exceed the limits of your physical capabilities and if you are in any doubt, exercise caution. If you are in charge of others, do not expect them to perform as you would. Moderation in all things should be your guide.

Your easy-going nature gives others the opportunity to take advantage of you. In this respect you would do well to seek an advisor. A close friend that you trust is probably the best bet.

Sufficient rest is essential for you to maintain good health and general well-being. Avoid excess in all things.

MAJOR COMPETITIONS

1971
Bulgaria
FRIENDSHIP CUP
GOLD – bars, beam
1973
East Germany
FRIENDSHIP CUP
OVERALL GOLD
GOLD – bars, vault
1975
England
CHAMPIONS ALL
OVERALL WINNER
Skien, Norway
EUROPEAN CHAMPIONSHIPS
OVERALL GOLD
GOLD – bars, beam, vault
SILVER – floor
Montreal, Canada
PRE-OLYMPICS
OVERALL WINNER
GOLD – bars
SILVER – vault, floor
BRONZE – beam
1976
USA
AMERICAN CUP
OVERALL WINNER
Montreal, Canada
OLYMPIC GAMES
OVERALL GOLD
GOLD – bars, beam
TEAM SILVER
BRONZE – floor
Nagoya, Japan
CHUNICHI CUP
OVERALL WINNER
GOLD – bars, beam, vault, floor
Salonika, Greece
BALKAN CHAMPIONSHIPS

OVERALL WINNER
GOLD – bars, beam, vault, floor

1977
Prague, Czechoslovakia
EUROPEAN CHAMPIONSHIPS
OVERALL GOLD
JOINT GOLD – bars
SILVER – vault
team withdrawn
1978
Strasbourg, France
WORLD CHAMPIONSHIPS
GOLD – beam
SILVER – vault
TEAM SILVER
1979
England
CHAMPIONS ALL
OVERALL WINNER
Copenhagen, Denmark
EUROPEAN CHAMPIONSHIPS
OVERALL GOLD
GOLD – valut, floor
BRONZE – beam
Tokyo, Japan
WORLD CUP
GOLD – vault, floor
SILVER – beam
Fort Worth, USA
WORLD CHAMPIONSHIPS
TEAM GOLD MEDAL
withdrew due to injury
1980
Moscow
OLYMPIC GAMES
GOLD – beam, floor (joint)
OVERALL SILVER
TEAM SILVER